The HAMPTONS HEALTH SPA DIET COOKBOOK

Based upon the Cuisine developed by the authors for the International Health & Beauty Spa at Gurney's Inn, Montauk, N.Y.

illustration and design by MICHAEL J. SMOLLIN

The HAMPTONS HEALTH SPA DIET COOKBOOK

FLORENCE KULICK
and
FLORENCE MATTHEWS

The Permanent Press
Sag Harbor N.Y. 11963

adipogenesis

In ancient days the pagan maid
   Who wanted to get thinner,
An offering near an idol laid,
   As though she were a sinner.

She prayed the gods would make her grow
   As slim as Aphrodite;
But gods are hard of hearing, so
   Her weight remained one-ninety.

Now times have changed and science is
   The newest god created,
To whom the scientific miss
   Appeals when overweighted.

With learned prattle she declaims
   That carbohydrates fatten;
She glibly rattles off their names
   And chemistry in latin.

You may be sure she understands
   The most perplexing diet;
The action of the ductless glands
   To stimulate or quiet.

She talks so much of diets that
   You weary of her chatter,
For you can see she's still as fat—
   If not a little fatter.

She reads and swallows every ad
   On nostrums for reducing;
And follows every current fad
   That quacks are introducing.

The easy way to slenderize
   No science but a farce is.
It melts her down to modest size
   By strong saline catharsis.

One method though she'll never choose—
   Because her will's too fleeting;
She'll do 'most anything to lose,
   Except to give up eating.

Nicholas G. Demy, M.D.
1932

Library of Congress Catalogue Number: 82-084011

International Standard Book Number: 0-932966-28-4

THE PERMANENT PRESS
Sag Harbor, New York 11963

Printed in the United States of America

contents

acknowledgements

We acknowledge with thanks and appreciation our students, our many friends and our loving husbands who participated in the kitchen testing of all the recipes in this book.

We also thank Joyce and Nick Monte, of Gurney's Inn, as well as Gisella Waterman, and the chefs and staff of their International Health and Beauty Spa for their confidence in our cuisine and cooking methods. They earned our deep respect and appreciation when we invaded their kitchens to install our Hamptons Diet in the Spa.

Our special appreciation to Clyde Matthews for his help and inspiration in launching this book, and to Bernard Kulick for his mathematical calculations, and to both of our husbands for their forbearance in our endeavor.

Special thanks to Judy and Martin Shepard, our editors and publishers, for their suggestions and to our super friend, Jinx Walker, for getting our manuscript into shape.

foreword

It is difficult to find a first time dieter — the individual who has never dieted before. There are untold numbers of diet plans, and yet the vast majority of dieters are unsuccessful. There are innumerable diet scams. As a result, today's dieter is barraged with quick weight loss diet schemes, buffeted by conflicting opinions as to what is and what is not important, and certainly confused by frequently inadequate and incomplete advice.

There are diets that produce very quick weight loss, but are most likely to result in regaining lost weight. There are diets that "work," but are medically unsafe. There are diets that look good on paper but are difficult to follow, or use recipes that are impractical or unappealing. Of course, there are always diets that are ineffective from the start.

The most important aspect of a sound diet is medical safety. Tampering with one's health certainly defeats every benefit of any diet. We have considerable knowledge of the safety factors in nutrition: the proper balance of protein and carbohydrates; a good vitamin and mineral content; avoidance of cholesterol and saturated fats; and a marked limitation of sugar and salt. These nutritional guidelines have been clearly stated by many official health agencies such as the American Heart Association, as well as the Select Committee on Human Nutrition of the United States Senate. *The Hamptons Health Spa Diet Cookbook* places all these factors into proper balance.

Obviously, a good diet requires effective caloric control. The essential ingredient of caloric control is fat control, accomplished by careful menu selection and recipe development. The ultimate goal of any weight loss program is that the diet must allow one to keep weight loss permanently, perpetually, constantly! This can be accomplished in only one way. It is the permanent development of sound eating habits. This should probably be written in capital and italics as well as underlined. The development of these habits is the *only* way known to stay thinner permanently.

The *Hamptons Health Spa Diet* has addressed itself to effective weight loss, to safe and healthy weight loss, and to the development of sound eating habits for long term slimness. It has done this soundly and sensibly and deserves very high marks indeed for its nutritional expertise. This book offers a very sophisticated way to diet successfully. It includes recipes that have a special appeal because they also provide a delectable way to diet. *The Hamptons Health Spa Diet Cookbook* is a cookbook with a real purpose and a well accomplished one.

Getting thin forever need not be elusive, it need not be unsafe, and the *Hamptons Health Spa Diet Cookbook* is a delightful and medically recommended way to do it.

Morton B. Glenn, M.D.
Past President of the American College of Nutrition.
Assistant Professor of Clinical Medicine
at the New York University School of Medicine,
and consultant to the Bureau of Nutrition, New York City Department of Health.

introduction

Another diet book, you say. We believe it is much more: a diet book, a nutrition book, a cookbook — all integrated into one healthy, vibrant-lifestyle book.

The *Hamptons Health Spa Diet Cookbook* was conceived and hatched in East Hampton, New York. The recipes and menus were tested in Southampton, demonstrated regularly on East Hampton cable TV, and incorporated in one of the country's outstanding health spas at Montauk.

The concept grew out of fifteen years of research into the most advanced findings of the nutritional and medical communities. We derived its inspiration from the dynamic lifestyle of the active, sophisticated Hamptonites who summer and live year-round in the beautiful South Fork resort villages and towns of Long Island's East End. Here some of the country's most talented and successful people — in the arts, sciences, business and the professions — live, play and entertain smartly and graciously. As a group they are very conscious of both their looks and health, and have turned the joy of living into an art form which is greatly admired around the country.

The *Hamptons Health Spa Diet* is a nutritional cuisine which reflects this lifestyle. Its purpose is to bring slimness, buoyant health and a sense of well-being to those who wish it, without sacrificing the *haute cuisine* which makes dining such a pleasure. It is low in calories, fats and oils, cholesterol, sugar and salt — all those elements traditionally considered essential to gourmet dishes. Our diet features many delectable international recipes — spanakopita, tandoori fish, blini, coquilles, fettuccini, moussaka — that are low in those damaging ingredients, but high in taste.

We believe this diet will delight you, your family and your friends. You will look and feel much better because our nutritional approach will not only enable you to lose weight effectively, it will improve your health and keep you looking fit and attractive. It will also do wonders for your mental outlook. Overall, it provides a lifetime basis for a gourmet diet based upon sound nutrition.

This is not a fad diet on which you lose weight quickly, but put it on again just as fast; it is not a diet that depends on food substitutes such as saccharine for sugar or potassium chloride for salt; nor one featuring prepared food products that contain so many additives you think you're feasting on a chemical smorgasbord; and it is not another lopsided diet that can impair your health.

The *Hamptons Health Spa Diet* has been tested by community groups, at innumerable East Hampton private parties, and at Southampton College adult classes. The cuisine of the noted International Health and Beauty Spa at Gurney's Inn in Montauk, Long Island, is based upon the diet and menu plan in this book. This cuisine has proven to be both popular and effective with the Spa's sophisticated clientele.

Those who frequent health spas will find this diet valuable to follow as a regular regimen, to extend the benefits of their going there. *Everyone* can capitalize on the *Hamp-*

tons Health Spa Diet for many of the same reasons one goes to a health spa: to achieve and maintain proper body weight and firmness, and to enjoy better health and improved good looks.

To help you start on your weight-loss, good-health plan, we have outlined a 14-Day Diet Plan. You will discover that it is possible to eat delectably, not be hungry, and still lose weight. And it is easy to continue, because you learn how to use the additional recipes in this book to create your own menus, using the 14-Day Plan as a guide.

The nutritional information will help you understand *why* it is important to eat healthfully. We believe this understanding is absolutely essential to energize your motivation.

The key to our diet plan is to lose weight *slowly* over a period of time, thereby giving you the opportunity to change your food habits. *When it comes to weight loss, slow, not fast, is the answer.* It is only by changing the way you think and act about food that will enable you to take weight off and keep it off. Rapid weight loss diets always boomerang because weight lost quickly is regained just as quickly. Crash diets are nutritionally unsound and often medically dangerous.

An important bonus of the *Hamptons Health Spa Diet* is its valuable side effects. Numerous medical studies have demonstrted that a diet low in fat, cholesterol, sugar and salt will not only keep your weight at a desirable level, it may also help avoid or alleviate heart disease, hypertension, diabetes and other medical problems. No one can guarantee it, but it may also help you live longer. Certainly the quality of your life should be improved.

This is a nutritional cuisine as much as a diet which, with some modification, you can stay on forever. Who's going to argue against staying slim, looking good, feeling great while dining deliciously? We hope you find this the best of all possible worlds.

weight control

Lose fifteen pounds in fourteen days, THEY say . . . WE say that's impossible. You will lose water pounds, not fat pounds. Even if you starved yourself and exercised for hours on end, you could not lost *FAT* that quickly. We plan to take you on the most sensible and effective route to weight control, the only method that works in the long run.

We will detour you around the pitfalls in the weight-game most Americans are playing, and help you take responsibility for proper management of your weight loss program. Our 14-Day Diet Plan opens the door to slow, steady, permanent FAT-pound loss.

Start by shedding negative images, such as "I'm built just like my mother, I'll always be overweight." Or, "I was a fat kid, I can't help myself." Even if you are built just like your mother or father, accept that part of the truth, but totally deny the rest. Even if you were a fat child and are stuck with fat cells, they don't have to be filled up. Start your own dynasty of slim, trim, nutritionally savvy people.

Our diet is a nutrient feast of exquisite food with reduced fat, sugar, salt, cholesterol and calories. It begins with a 14-Day Diet Plan based on high complex carbohydrates — whole grains, fruits and vegetables — and fish and fowl, with as little red meat as possible. Recent scientific reports confirm our approach, recommending reduced intake of fats and increased consumption of carbohydrates in belief that doing so can lessen the risk of cardio-vascular diseases and cancer. You don't have to subsist on celery sticks, carrot curls, bland broiled fish and fake jello to lose weight. Our exotic menus include ample breakfasts, lunches that leave you satisfied until evening, and enjoyable, luxurious dinners.

We build in good nutrition, good eating habits and leave you room for snacks of fruit. We give you bread and butter, potatoes, quiches, crepes and salads with tangy dressings. We offer you creamy soups and delicious chowders, tasty desserts and internationally famous main courses that would delight an epicure. Portion control is the key.

Is there any easy way to lose weight? NO!

Don't be lured into thinking that you can lose ten pounds in fourteen days and KEEP THEM OFF with no problem. Those water-loss pounds will return as quickly as you lose them. You *cannot* eat all you want and still lose weight. You *cannot* go on a lopsided diet for any length of time without paying a penalty. Fruit diets, high protein diets, high fat diets, starvation diets just are not safe. They are *not* the way to do it.

YOU CAN LOSE WEIGHT ON OUR DIET . . . BECAUSE:
1. You won't be hungry; our meals are satisfying.
2. You won't feel deprived. These meals can be shared with everyone. Your friends and family will never suspect that they are eating diet food. *You* must have a calorie-controlled portion, and those without a weight problem may eat larger portions.

3. You won't feel guilty if you occasionally binge. It happens to all of us. Forgive yourself and be prepared to pay back at the very next meal. Just get right back on your diet and deal with it the next time it happens.
4. You will not allow yourself to be sabotaged by your family and well-meaning friends. You will help them understand that you are committed to a new way of eating.
5. You won't be bored with this cuisine. These calorie-controlled meals are tasty, attractive and easy to prepare.
6. The book and methods described will help you focus on eating sensibly. Some diets urge you to not think about food, but we suggest that you do think about every morsel that you eat, and savor it.

SOME HELPFUL TECHNIQUES FOR STAYING ON THIS DIET
1. Eat slowly. You will enjoy it more and it has an important practical value, too. There is a small gland at the base of the brain called the hypothalmus that controls appetite. When you eat slowly, your appestat (the appetite control mechanism in your brain) has a chance to signal that you have had enough. Heed its message! If you eat too quickly, not enough time elapses for the brain to signal that it has enough for the moment, and you eat more than you should. Many people continue eating long after their appetites are satisfied.
2. If you feel the need for snacks, try:
    a. Salt-free tomato juice spiked with lemon or lime, pepper, etc.
    b. Salt-free, fat-free bouillon or one of our low calorie soups.
    c. Raw vegetables: celery, broccoli, cauliflower, pepper, carrots, cucumber, zucchini, etc.
    d. Hot drinks (marvelous for filling space) such as herbal teas, decaffeinated coffee, cambric tea (hot water and milk).
3. Keep candy, cakes, cookies, ice cream, pastries and other high-fat, high-salt, high-sugar snacks out of the house. It may seem childish, but it does help to know they just aren't there. Try popcorn made without fat or salt; it has only 25 calories for one-half cup.
4. Examine your own food tastes. If there are certain foods you crave, budget them in occasionally in small quantities. Don't wait until the desire builds up to bingeing proportions.
5. Divide your food intake into smaller, more frequent meals throughout the day, if it is easier for you to diet that way.
6. If you backslide off your diet, it is not a disaster. What is a disaster is not getting right back on.
7. The balance in our cuisine is important. Full meals are provided so that you can control intake. You must follow the suggested portions.

diet and exercise

There is more to losing weight than counting calories. Only a combination of diet and exercise can help you maintain a sustained weight loss and promote physical fitness. Regardless of your physical condition, there are exercises you can do to help your body function more efficiently and with less fatigue.

The well-upholstered ladies of Rubens' day are as passe as the consumptive, swooning, fragile Lady Camille types. Healthy, trim, vivacious good looks for both women and men are today's ideal, both medically and aesthetically.

REACHING A PLATEAU

After a few weeks of dieting, it is not unusual to reach a weight-loss plateau. You're not eating more than you think. Your metabolism (rate at which you burn food) is slowing down to adjust to the lowered caloric intake. It's nature's way of protecting itself. As you lose weight, fewer calories are needed to support your activities, so weight is lost more slowly. You will burn up a number of calories during exercise which in turn will stimulate your metabolism to continue to burn more calories long after you have finished exercising.

We know that dieting is no fun, and it is hard work. It can be very discouraging to find you are not losing weight at the same rate that you did when you started. You have simply arrived at a plateau which is a normal and frequent occurrence. Exercise is the only way to overcome it.

How you react when you reach a plateau can spell the difference between the success and failure of your diet. Once you pass this static situation, your weight loss will resume. It may take several days or as long as a week or two, but don't be disheartened or allow yourself to become depressed. Stick with your portion control and exercise program. Studies have shown this is the only to get past the plateau.

WHAT IS THE BEST WAY TO GET STARTED?
1. Select a time of day for exercising and try to plan the same time slot each day. A regularly scheduled time becomes part of your routine and stays with you. Never exercise directly after meals.
2. Select an aerobic exercise to stimulate your cardio-vascular system. Almost all medical studies recommend regular exercise as a lifestyle to help reduce the risk of heart disease. Blood vessels tend to thicken when you do not exercise, thus reducing their ability to carry an adequate blood supply to the heart. For those with cardio-vascular problems, exercise will help new blood vessels to gradually develop, building a collateral system. The theory is that a well-conditioned heart will have additional vessels to take over if and when there is a blockage. Walking and/or swimming are excellent ways to begin your exercise program.

3. Select exercises for improving muscle tone and flexibility. Stretching, bending and arm circles are good warm-ups for doing more vigorous exercises later on. Don't buy devices you see advertised for exercising your way to slimness. The only one who benefits is the manufacturer.

Once you have decided which exercises you are going to do, start slowly. Gradually build up the length of time and intensity of the exercises. Don't do too much too quickly. You don't want to end up with muscle aches and twinges of joint pain. Perserverance is the program, not Olympic competition.

We stress walking as one of the best ways to exercise because it can be done almost anywhere, any time, and needs no special equipment. Build up your pace slowly, but keep building. Walking at the rate of three miles per hour burns up 250 calories; it should take about 20 minutes to do a mile at this pace. At the rate of four miles per hour, or 15 minutes per mile, you will burn 350 calories.

You have to burn up 3500 calories to lose one pound of fat. It can best be done by a combination of diet and exercise. Reducing your caloric intake by 800 calories a day and walking for one hour (350 calories) will result in 1150 fewer calories daily and a weight loss of about 2 to 2½ pounds per week. So cut out that extra snack, and walk your mile. It's a simple matter of intake and output.

Fad diets usually promise miracles, and they may work on a short term basis. However, fast water-weight loss is evident only on the scale. Don't be deluded. It takes a slow, steady reduction of 3500 calories to lose a pound of FAT.

To tone up your muscles, try some of the following exercises. Work them in while doing other things. Repeat them several times and as often during the day as you can.

1. When driving a car or sitting at a desk, contract your abdominal muscles to the count of five and then relax to the count of five. Repeat several times. This is good for tightening your stomach muscles.
2. Tighten your buttocks while preparing a meal, doing housework, or washing the car.
3. Stretching is a surprisingly untapped source of exercise which feels good, strengthens your mid-section and improves your posture. Your mid-section is the key to holding your body erect.
4. To relax and firm your neck muscles, turn your head slowly to the right as far as you can, back to center and then to the left. Next, rotate your head in slow circles, first one way and then another. It's a good exercise to do while watching TV.
5. To maintain the range of motion of your shoulder joints and improve your posture, do several circles with your arms out-stretched, first in one direction and then the other.

Choices and combinations are endless. Just keep moving. Whether you decide to join a spa, do it on your own, or a combination of the two, the important thing is to get started. Exercise regularly to help maintain your weight loss, to get you through plateaus and to improve your cardio-vascular system. Remember, to achieve good muscle tone during weight loss, you must exercise.

Physical fitness is a total commitment which enables you to achieve the goal of feeling fit and healthy, looking good and giving you a measure of control over the quality of your own life.

nutrition

It is difficult to pick up a newspaper or magazine or listen to radio or TV without reading or hearing something about nutrition. It has become a fashionable buzz word at parties and discussions of nutrition among friends are common. While our consciousness has certainly been raised about the importance of good nutrition, what is heard is often simplistic, fragmentary, commercially self-serving or just plain inaccurate.

The only defense is to *know*. It doesn't take a degree in dietetics or nutrition. All it takes is *interest* in good cause: your health and your good looks. The nutritional information in this book will help you understand the importance and functions of various nutrients. *It is all the basic information you need to know, and it is worth learning!*

calories

Everything you eat or drink, except water, has calories. A calorie is a unit of heat energy. It is the fuel our bodies need in order to function. Even at rest, your body uses calories for breathing, blood circulation, digestion and other basic needs. That is your basic metabolism. Your only sources of energy (calories) are protein, fat, and carbohydrate (starch and sugar). To help you understand how caloric values are arrived at, look at the following chart:

1 gm. carbohydrate	= 4 calories
1 gm. protein	= 4 calories
1 gm. fat	= 9 calories

(There are 28.5 gms. in one ounce.)

To calculate how many calories there are in one-half cup of one-half percent fat cottage cheese, the nutrients are broken down as follows:

4 gms. carbohydrate	× 4	= 16 calories
14 gms. protein	× 4	= 56 calories
1 gm. fat	× 9	= 9 calories
	Total	= 80 calories in ½ cup.

This information is now given on most canned and packaged goods. Food labels have become much more informative in recent years because of the pressure brought by consumer groups on government agencies and food manufacturers.

How many calories does one need per day?

That depends on your age, sex, bone structure, height, weight and activity. There are many charts to guide you, but the average female in an occupation that is largely sedentary needs about 1800 calories daily to maintain normal weight, while a man in a similar capacity needs about 2400. You don't have to worry about calories if your weight stays within a normal range. But remember, a mere two extra pounds a year can add up. An acceptable long-range weight loss program can be accomplished with 1200 calories for women and 1500 for men until the desired weight goal is reached. On a short-range basis this can be reduced to 1,000 calories and 1200 respectively.

carbohydrates

Why are sugars and startches lumped together under the broad heading of carbohydrates?

These are included in the same category because both starches and sugars are broken down by the body into simple sugars as the end products of digestion.

Why is sugar so severely limited on this diet?

Refined sugar (sucrose) has absolutely no positive nutritional value. It provides empty calories, ruins teeth, irritates the lining of the digestive tract and may lead to diabetes in later life. Many medical researchers feel that triglycerides, a fat produced when the body has an excess amount of sugar, can be just as bad, if not worse, than cholesterol in its effect on heart disease.

Unfortunately, sugar is an ever-present and over-abundant substance in many prepared foods. Read every label. You will find hidden sugar in places you least suspect: ketchup, tomato sauce, bread, prepared cereals, just to name a few.

Take a look at the sugar in some of the common foods you eat.

Food	Sugar Calories	Total Calories
1 donut, plain, 3½"	16	200
½ pt. ice cream	68	136
1 portion Jello	75	82
1 tsp. jelly	16	20
1 Tbsp. ketchup	9	19
2 peach halves plus 1 Tbsp. syrup	14	65
1 oz. raisin bran	48	110
1 tsp. sugar	16	16

Would it be better to substitute honey for sugar?

Although honey may not be as irritating to the digestive tract as sugar, it is so easily digested that its effect on the body is the same. Don't be fooled by all the health food and natural food ads. Raw sugar, turbinado sugar or honey all have the same effect on the body, and the nutrients contained in them is minimal. Food manufacturers are quick to capitalize on the current honey fad and are now adding it to many products, such as honeyed cereals. If you like honey, by all means, use it, but use it as sparingly as sugar. Honey is sweeter than sugar, so use less of it.

Why are whole grains being stressed so much in recent years?

Whole grains provide vitamins, minerals and fiber which cannot be found in any enriched white flour products. Another advantage is that they digest more slowly and as a result the body can use the glucose (sugar) more efficiently because it is fed into the bloodstream more slowly. You can liken the digestion of carbohydrate to water running into a sink. If the water runs in slowly, it will run freely down the drain. If it runs in too quickly, the sink will begin to fill up because the drain pipe cannot handle the sudden volume. The same thing happens in your body. If the food takes longer to digest, the glucose, which is the end product of carbohydrate digestion, will be fed into the bloodstream more slowly and evenly. If it digests too quickly, too much gets into the bloodstream at once and the body cannot handle it efficiently. The excess is converted to fat.

fiber

Fiber is the indigestible part of food, primarily plant food. The greatest amount of fiber can be found in raw fruits, such as apples and bananas; raw vegetables like lettuce, cucumbers, celery and carrots; cooked vegetables such as potatoes, eggplant, beans; whole grains, like oatmeal. An assortment of fruits and vegetables, as well as whole grains will provide you with the fiber necessary for good health.

How is fiber important?

It is particularly valuable in the digestive process to help avoid constipation. Some recent research has indicated that fiber may also be helpful in reducing cholesterol levels, and perhaps in lowering the rate of cancer of the bowel. However, although it has had a renaissance in recent years, it is certainly not the cure-all some experts would have you believe.

Should raw bran be added to the diet?

It is not necessary to add bran if you eat the proper foods, such as whole grains, fruits and vegetables. Adding fiber in the form of bran may cause too rapid elimination, thus depriving the body of some of the essential elements it needs. This is one time when too much of a good thing may be harmful. Food manufacturers, trying to take advantage of the current interest in fiber, are beginning to add bran to cereals and bread. Only you can judge if it is too much for your system. If you do add bran, start slowly and use the bran without added sugar. In some breads and cereals, wood pulp is being added, which can be constipating. Again, read your labels carefully.

Are there any disadvantages to fiber?

Some people find themselves very gaseous as they switch to a more fibrous diet, especially with certain vegetables such as cabbage, brussel sprouts, and members of the bean family. Add fibrous foods slowly in order to adjust easily.

fat

Fat, whether it comes in a solid form like butter or in a liquid form as oil, provides more than twice as many calories as protein or carbohydrates. It is easy to understand why fat is fattening.

According to the latest figures*, a large proportion of our population is still consuming more than 40% of their diet in fat, which leads to weight problems for many people. The majority of medical opinion today feels that this is dangerous because fat, particularly saturated fat, along with cholesterol, contributes to cardio-vascular disease. Recent government dietary standards suggest limiting fat intake to 30%* of your diet. Our cuisine limits fat to 20%.

Some of the difficulty in lowering fat consumption is due to the fact that fat is not always visible as fat. It's easy to recognize butter, margarine, oil and mayonnaise as fat, but it is not so visible in meat, luncheon meats, eggs, cheese, whole milk, cream, and nuts. Fat is also a prominent ingredient in all kinds of desserts, pastries and many prepared foods.

What are the different types of fat?

There are three types of fat:
    Saturated
    Monosaturated
    Unsaturated

An easy way to remember the differences is that saturated fats are solid at room temperature, and unsaturated and monosaturated fats are liquid at room temperature. No fat is completely saturated and no fat is completely unsaturated. Medical opinion today believes that saturated fats tend to raise the cholesterol level of the blood while unsaturated fat lowers it. Monosaturated fats seem to have no effect either way.

*See appendix.

Saturated Fat
Foods of animal origin as meat, butter, egg yolks, whole milk and cheese are high in saturated fat. Poultry has less saturated fat than red meat and fish even less than poultry. Since saturated fats tend to raise the cholesterol level of the blood, our cuisine concentrates on fish, poultry, skim milk and a few eggs. These are also lower in calories than foods high in saturated fats.

Some fats of vegetable origin, such as coconut oil and palm oil, are highly saturated. That is why all those cream substitutes such as whipped toppings, imitation sour cream and substitute milk which use coconut oil as a base are such poor choices. In addition, they have many chemical additives and should be avoided. Unfortunately, palm and coconut oils are ever-present in prepared foods, particularly cakes, cookies and prepared mixes. *Read your labels.*

Monosaturated Fat
These fats have no apparent effect on cholesterol levels but they are still fat, 100% fat. Olive oil is a monosaturated fat. We do not use it in our cuisine, preferring a polyunsaturated oil in a *very limited* quantity for its possible beneficial effect of lowering cholesterol.

Unsaturated Fats
Fats of vegetable origin are referred to as oil or polyunsaturated oil. The higher the percentage of polyunsaturates in an oil, the better, since they tend to lower the cholesterol level of the blood. In descending order, the most desirable are:

Safflower Oil
Sesame Oil
Corn Oil
Peanut Oil

When oil is changed from a liquid to a solid, it becomes saturated. Cans of shortening used for baking and frying have been "hydrogenated," which means that it has become a *saturated* fat, even though it is of vegetable origin. Heating the oil or frying at high temperatures also saturates the oil.

How does margarine compare with butter?
Margarines, although made from vegetable oil, become more saturated when converted to a solid form and some are no different than butter in that respect. Some margarine labels tell you the number of grams of saturates and unsaturates in that particular product. Margarines do not contain cholesterol, but they do contain chemical ad-

ditives. Some contain salt and all are FAT. Butter and margarine both have the same caloric value per tablespoon, 100 calories. Whipped butters and margarines have fewer calories per portion because water and air have been added.

Since butter contains cholesterol and margarines contain additives, we can make no recommendation other than severely limiting whichever you decide to use.

What limits does our diet place on fat?

Our cuisine has no more than 20% fat, keeping a balance between saturates and poly-unsaturates. We believe that by keeping the fat intake at 20% or less, there will still be enough fat for all the necessary bodily functions; your hair and skin will stay well-lubricated, your weight will more readily remain at a normal level, and it will help prevent degenerative diseases.

How much fat is there in the foods we commonly eat?

On a 1,000-1,200 calorie diet, about 200-240 *fat* calories would represent 20% of your daily caloric intake.

A quick look at the following chart will show you how quickly fat calories add up.

Food	Fat Calories	Total Calories
1 oz. American cheese	90	105
½ medium avocado	144	167
1 brownie 2″ × 2″	32	180
4 oz. lean beef, raw, fillet	99	208
1 Tbsp. butter or margarine	100	100
4 oz. chicken (white) raw	36	188
4 oz. lean fish, raw, fillet	33	90
1 oz. peanuts, shelled	112	180
1 Tbsp. oil	120	120
1 chocolate chip cookie, 1″ diam.	27	55
1 slice cheesecake, 1/8 cake, cream cheese base	288	400
1 donut, 3½″ diam.	99	225

Favorite snacks and appetizers at parties are cheese, sour cream dips, nuts and quiches. Before the meal even begins, you have used up your quota of fat, and when you add the dessert, you have gone way over the limit.

cholesterol

Cholesterol has become a buzz word in recent years and much controversy surrounds it. Cholesterol is not a fat, but a waxy substance known as a sterol. It is found in animal foods and, like fat, does not dissolve in water. It is a necessary component of all tissues of the body. Cholesterol has been identified as an element, along with fat, that is involved in the building up of plaque in the arteries.

Cholesterol is manufactured by the body, and is also taken in with animal fatty foods. Some people have a high cholesterol count without eating any real amount of animal fatty foods (saturated fats); others eat an enormous amount of "wrong foods" and have a low cholesterol count. The debates and controversy center around the extent to which the cholesterol level of the blood can be controlled through diet.

Enough studies have been done to at least show a causal relationship between the amount of cholesterol in the bloodstream with the subsequent plaque build-up in the arteries to convince us that is wise to limit the amount of cholesterol-rich foods in your diet.

What about eggs?

Eggs have a great deal of cholesterol, but they also contain lecithin. Some researchers say the lecithin breaks up the fat and cholesterol molecules in the yolk so that it can be handled readily by the body. There is not that much evidence to support this view, so again, we advise you to limit the intake of eggs to 2-3 per week. Use egg-whites in baking and cooking, and eliminate the cholesterol-rich yolk wherever you can.

Are fat and cholestrol the same?

NO! Some foods may be low in fat, but high in cholesterol, such as shrimp, lobster and most shellfish. A food can also be low in calories, but high in cholesterol, such as eggs and liver.

Foods from animal sources contain saturated fats and cholesterol. Foods of vegetable origin contain unsaturated fat and no cholesterol. Palm and coconut oil are the exceptions since they contain saturated fat, but no cholesterol.

What are high and low density lipids?

In order for lipids (fats) to be transported in the bloodstream, the must combine with proteins to form lipoproteins. Very low density lipids and low density lipids are considered the "bad guys" because they keep cholesterol and triglycerides in circulation. High density lipids, the "good guys," aid in the removal of cholesterol from the tissues. Recent research has shown that those people with a greater proportion of high density lipids seem to have greater protection against heart disease. To what extent diet can help is not clear, but exercise does seem to help in increasing the high density lipids. This is an area of research worth watching.

How much cholesterol is there in the foods we commonly eat?

Food	Mg.* Cholesterol
1 oz. butter	71
1 oz. cheese	25
1 egg yolk	250
4 oz. fish	55-75
4 oz. raw liver	497
4 oz. raw meat	75-100
1 8-oz. glass of milk	34
4 oz. poultry (with skin)	80
(without skin)	60
4 oz. shirmp	170

Our diet averages less than 300 mg. per day.**

*Note: There are 1,000 milligrams in one gram, and cholesterol is measured in milligrams.

**See appendix

protein

Every cell in the body needs protein. Life could not be sustained without it. Protein is needed to build and repair tissue, regulate water balance, manufacture enzymes, hormones and antibodies and is also burned for energy. You need some protein every day because the nitrogen in protein cannot be stored.

Are some proteins better than others?

Proteins are broken down into amino acids as the end products of digestion. Proteins from animal sources, such as meat, poultry, fish, milk, cheese and eggs are considered "higher quality" proteins because they contain all the essential amino acids necessary for building and repairing tissue.

Proteins from vegetable sources are considered "lower quality" because they contain only some of the essential amino acids. However, eating a cereal grain with a bean product at the same meal will result in the proper combination of amino acids. Many ethnic diets combine these foods in delicious dishes such as rice and beans of the Mexicans (Refritos and Rice), and pasta and beans of the Italians (Pasta Fazool).

How much protein do we need?

Not as much as you think—only about one gram for every 2.2 lbs. of normal body weight. For the average woman that means about 50-60 grams of protein and for the average man, about 60-70 grams.

A look at the following chart will show you how quickly that adds up.

Food	Grams Protein
2 slices bread	4
½ cup cooked beans	8
4 oz. cottage cheese (½ cup)	7
1 oz. hard cheese	7
1 egg white (protein in white only)	4
3 oz. cooked meat or fish	24-28
1 glass milk (skim or whole)	9
2 oz. pasta	7

With six ounces of animal protein foods, plus one glass of milk and some bread, your day's needs will be fulfilled. If you prefer not to eat meat or fish, some milk, cheese, pasta, beans and bread will do just as well.

Are there any dangers in high protein diets?

Americans have had a romance with protein. They have been brought up to think that a large amount of animal protein is healthy. Large portions of meat, eggs, whole milk and hard cheeses were considered essential. That thinking is now changing because so many animal foods are also high in saturated fat, cholesterol and calories.

Many high protein diets are considered dangerous over a long period of time because the nitrogen in protein is eliminated daily, and an excessive amount puts a strain on the liver and kidneys. That's why these diets advise you to drink so many glasses of water. Since the body is not being supplied with enough carbohydrates on these diets, the protein will be burned for energy. We agree with drinking lots of water daily, but you certainly don't need all that protein.

sodium

Sodium chloride, or salt, as it is commonly known, contains 40% sodium. Sodium is an essential ingredient of all body fluids, tissues, and cells, but only a very small amount is needed, about 200 mg. daily. Sodium in excess of that is left to be eliminated by the kidneys, placing a strain on this vital organ. Too much sodium is also a contributing cause of high blood pressure (hypertension). If there is an existing heart or kidney malfunction, sodium may accumulate in the tissues and water is retained with a resulting strain on the heart.

Is the salt content listed on food labels?

Unfortunately, most labels indicate that salt is present, but not the amount. If salt is listed among the first three ingredients, you can be sure that there is *too much* salt. Read your labels. Understand the importance of the information and reject high salt content foods. Sea salt and rock salt are still salt. The following chart shows the sodium content of some commonly used foods.

Food	Mg. Sodium
Beef, 4 oz.	120-160
Bouillon cube, 1	960
Bread, 1 regular slice	120-160
Cheese	
American, 1 oz.	320
Cottage, ¼ cup	225
Swiss, 1 oz.	200
Cheese spread, 1 oz.	400
Condiments & Sauces	
Catsup, 1 Tbsp.	263
Horseradish, 1 oz.	312
Mayonnaise, 1 Tbsp.	84
Mustard, 1 tsp.	60
Salad dressing, 1 tbsp.	165-300
Soy sauce, 1 Tbsp.	1200
Worcestershire sauce, 1 Tbsp.	150
Milk, 8 oz.	125
Salt, 1 tsp.	2000
Soup, canned, 1 cup	800-900
Soup, dried, 1 cup	1000
Tomatoes, ½ cup canned	145
Tomato juice, ½ cup	245

Sodium is found naturally in almost all foods, but in small quantities. Almost all processed foods contain salt which is why we severely limit them. We do not recommend the use of salt substitutes since the effect of their use over an extended period of time is not known. We suggest that you use a salt substitute *only* upon the advice of your physician. Potassium chloride is used as a substitute for salt in many low sodium products. We do not add salt per se. We use herbs, seasonings and fruits to charm your taste buds away from salt. Salt is a learned taste. It may take some time to wean yourself away from it, but you will find your appreciation for good food a lot keener without the hazard of salt. Our menus contain under 2000 mg. of sodium per day.*

*See appendix

vitamins

While we know a great deal more about the functions of vitamins each year, there is still continuing disagreement among authorities as to whether vitamin supplements should be taken and in what amounts.

Vitamins are diminished by the addition of chemicals to the soil, by the over-processing of foods, by the mode and time involved in transportation and refrigeration, and by the use of additives. When we finally do purchase our foods, there is also a marked effect on the amount of vitamins retained by food because of the way in which it is prepared; over-cooking, over-long freezing and long storage under refrigeration decreases vitamin content.

Are vitamin supplements advisable?

We do not recommend vitamin supplements unless they are prescribed by a physician. We firmly believe it is more beneficial to obtain vitamins through a proper diet. Our nutritionally balanced meals, properly prepared will afford you the right amount of vitamins. Do not get caught up in the false assumption that as long as you take vitamin supplements, you can skip many basic foods. In any case, most foods are certainly more interesting and satisfying than popping pills. And who knows what new vitamins scientists will discover in the future?

Are some vitamins more important than others?

All vitamins are important, each one serving a different purpose. There are two kinds of vitamins, the fat-soluble and the water-soluble vitamins.

The Fat-Soluble Vitamins: A,D,E,K

The fat-soluble vitamins can be stored in the body over long periods of time. It is important not to take an excessive quantity of these vitamins. It has been found that excessive amounts of A and D vitamins can be toxic.

Vitamin A: necessary for normal vision and to keep skin tone healthy. Food sources: whole milk, butter, egg yolk, cheese, yellow and dark green leafy vegetables, apricots, cantaloupe and peaches.

Vitamin D: necessary for calcium absorption, to help maintain strong bones. Food sources: fortified milk and all fortified milk products.

Vitamin E: prevents destruction of fatty acids and protects your intake of vitamin A. Maintains red blood cell membranes.

We have known about vitamin E for a long time, but since it is easily obtainable in foods, little attention had been paid to it. In recent years, some researchers have claimed that vitamin E can help prevent attacks of angina and can be generally helpful for cardiovascular patients. Studies in the United States have not yet confirmed these claims. Vitamin E oil has also been used successfully for some skin conditions and burn victims.

A great deal of work is also being done on the relationship between vitamin E and aging. There is nothing definitive yet. Will the fountain of youth be found in this vitamin? Food sources: vegetable oils, wheat germ, nuts, whole grains, green vegetables, meat.

Vitamin K: necessary for normal clotting of blood. Food sources: green leafy vegetables, cauliflower.

The Water-Soluble Vitamins: C,B Complex

Water-soluble vitamins are readily lost in cooking. Vitamin C is most unstable, being lost on exposure to air as well as in cooking.

B-Vitamins: Found in whole grains, dark green leafy vegetables, meat. They can be identified by names or numbers:

Thiamin	Pantothenic Acid
Riboflavin	Folic Acid
Niacin	Biotin
B-6	B-12

The dark outer leaves of lettuce should not be discarded. The darker green or yellow the vegetable, the higher the vitamin content. Include green vegetables in your diet daily.

Because of our weight-conscious orientation, many people have given up essential breads and cereals. They are losing an excellent source of B vitamins. By all means, include bread and cereal in your daily diet and make it whole grain. It's the butter you put on bread an pastas that make them so fattening. Although the government requires that refined flour be enriched with some B vitamins and iron, many natural values of the whole grain have been lost. Some vitamins, minerals and fiber have been refined out.

Vitamin C: Ascorbic acid is found in citrus fruits, strawberries, cantaloupe, tomatoes, pepper, cabbage, broccoli and potatoes.

Research into the possibility that vitamin C may prevent colds is still underway. Some studies show a decrease in the number and duration of colds through the use of this vitamin. However, there is disagreement about how much may be taken, and there is still not enough data on what effect an excess of vitamin C might have on health. The excess must be excreted by the kidneys and there is a possibility of stress on that vital organ. It is easy, pleasant and just plain smart to include a citrus fruit, a raw green vegetable along with many other choices of fruits and vegetables high in vitamin C, instead of taking a supplement.

minerals

Minerals, like vitamins, do not give the body energy, but are necessary for many body functions. Calcium and phosphorus have long been associated in the minds of the public with good bones and teeth, iron with good red blood, iodine with the prevention of goiter, potassium for the heart, and sodium for the tissues. Of course, this is an over-simplification, since each one of these minerals has many functions. In recent years, certain trace elements like zinc, magnesium, silenium, chromium, copper and fluorine have been added to the list of necessary minerals. Very small amounts of these minerals are necessary for health and they are readily obtainable in a well-balanced diet.

Are some minerals more important than others?
They are all important, but some are more difficult to obtain than others, particularly iron. Iron is found in small quantities if food—such as green vegetables, dried fruits, egg yolks, whole grains and meat. Where nature has been generous, as in organ meats and egg yolks, the cholesterol content is quite high. One of the reasons people have so much difficulty obtaining iron is that in attempting to reduce calories, they have eliminated or severely curtailed their consumption of bread and cereals. Although these foods contain relatively small amounts of iron, several slices a day add up, and we need all the iron we can get. Women may need an iron supplement.

Should mineral supplements be used?
As with vitamins, we do not feel that supplements are necessary if you have a properly balanced diet. What is important is preparing foods so that minerals are not lost in the cooking process. This will be covered under the food preparation section.

caffeine

"Until I have that cup of coffee in the morning, I can't get going," is a cliche describing a very common syndrome. The caffeine in coffee serves as a stimulant and can readily be classified as a drug. In fact, if you look at the label of some of the headache remedies, you will find caffeine as a key ingredient.

How much caffeine is there in various beverages?
While coffee is the major source of caffeine for Americans, many people consume substantial amounts of caffeine in soft drinks, tea, and other products. The following table reviews the main caffeine-containing products other than soft drinks. The caffeine

values listed are typical amounts derived from several sources, including Consumer Union tests, scientific literature, and standard reference works. Where appropriate, examples of specific brands are included.

Product	Caffeine (in milligrams)
Coffee	
Drip (5 oz.)	146
Percolated (5 oz.)	110
Instant, regular (5 oz.)	53
Decaffeinated (5 oz.)	2
Tea	
One-minute brew (5 oz.)	9 to 33
Three-minute brew (5 oz.)	20 to 46
Five-minute brew (5 oz.)	20 to 50
Canned ice tea (12 oz.)	22 to 36
Cocoa and chocolate	
Cocoa beverage (water mix, 6 oz.)	10
Milk chocolate (1 oz.)	6
Baking chocolate (1 oz.)	35
Nonprescription drugs	
Stimulants (standard dose)	
Caffedrine Capsules	200
NoDox Tablets	200
Vivarin Tablets	200
Pain relievers (standard dose)	
Anacin	64
Excedrin	130
Midol	65
Plain aspirin, any brand	0
Diuretics (standard dose)	
Aqua-Ban	200
Permathene H_2Off	200
Pre-Mens Forte	100
Cold remedies (standard dose)	
Coryban-D	30
Dristan	32
Triaminicin	30
Weight-control aids (daily dose)	
Dexatrim	200

Dietac	200
Prolamine	280

Why are we cautioned against too much caffeine?

Caffeine is a stimulant which speeds up the heart rate. This can be especially dangerous for people with heart problems. Some people have experienced heart palpitations after only one cup of coffee.

The coffee break that is so popular in industry today may give a person a temporary lift, but it has its drawbacks. The caffeine in the coffee and the sugar in the cake both stimulate the production of insulin, and after a brief spurt in the level of blood sugar, that level falls, giving you a let-down feeling.

Caffeine also stimulates the production of stomach acids and some people may experience heartburn after drinking coffee. People who have any type of stomach problems should avoid coffee, regular or decaffeinated.

Television and radio commercials have made us aware of the nervousness that may accompany the use of too much caffeine as well as the fact that sleeplessness may result. This, of course, is due to the stimulating effect that caffeine has on the nervous system.

Many gynecologists are also advising their patients with fibrocystic tendencies to avoid coffee as the caffeine increases the size and number of these breast masses which can turn cancerous.

What about decaffeinated coffee?

Decaffeinated coffee eliminates the caffeine problem, but there is some question about the safety of the chemicals used to eliminate the caffeine. Water washed decaffeinated beans are available in some stores.

What about tea?

The amount of caffeine in tea will depend upon its strength. Since tea can generally be drunk weaker than coffee, there is less caffeine per cup. It is a good idea to add milk to the tea, as the English do, to offset the effect of tannic acid.

In recent years, some people have been switching to herb teas, but there are questions about their safety, too. We must remember that tribal doctors used teas for medicinal purposes and we do not yet know the effect of the regular use of these teas. Check to see that the herb teas you use do not contain caffeine.

Do you recommend any particular beverage?

We make no recommendations other than keeping the caffeine to a minimum. Sodas are not advised because of their sugar or saccharine content, and colas contain caffeine in addition to sugar. It's amazing how many parents will not allow their children to drink coffee, but will give them cola drinks.

There are some cereal-based beverages on the market and you might like to try one. Europeans drink *cafe au lait*, which is mainly milk with a little bit of coffee. This might be an answer for some people. In any case, drink water. It's a great thirst quencher and it has zero calories. If you want a drink with a fizz, use seltzer that has no salt added.

additives

The first reaction of many people to additives is, "Eliminate them." But there are many different types of additives some of which, like vitamins and minerals, are used for nutritive purposes. We feel these additives are acceptable. Other additives are used for preservation, to enhance appearance or to aid in the processing or preparation of food and are of questionable safety. Anything that is added to the basic food in preparing it for canning or packaging is considered an additive. Salt and sugar are additives.

There has been an increased consciousness on the part of the public about additives as a result of recently published books and articles pointing out the dangers of many additives. The Food and Drug Administration (FDA), the watchdog government agency, has been accused of being too lenient about allowing the use of these additives. There are clear health hazards caused by food coloring, nitrates, monosodium glutamate and other chemicals because of their cancer-causing properties. There are many unanswered questions regarding additives. How does the body process them? Is a strain being placed on the organs that have to eliminate them? Are they stored in the body? Do they interact with other nutrients? Do they affect the absorption of essential foodstuffs? Scientists still do not know all the answers.

The FDA points to the fact that some preservatives are necessary to prevent food poisoning, but are so many necessary? BHA and BHT, for example, increase shelf life, but some cereals are packaged without them. With more and more consumer awareness, an increasing number of packaged goods are coming to the market without added preservatives. In our food preparation, we try to use as many fresh foods as possible. When we do use packaged or canned goods, we are careful to select water pac varieties, thus eliminating the oil as a general caveat, look for low salt and no preservative products. There is a new line of low salt products on the market which can be found on the regular shelves at the same prices as those that do have salt.

Selections From Basic Food Groups
To Satisfy Your Nutritional Needs

I. MILK AND DAIRY PRODUCTS — 2 servings per day

A.   **MILK**

Skim Milk: fat free, fresh or powdered. If you prepare the powdered skim milk a few hours in advance, it will develop a better flavor. Chill and you'll hardly notice the difference. It is a less expensive source of milk, satisfactory and excellent for cooking. You will be saving about 60 calories with each cup.

Evaporated skim milk: also fat free, found only in cans. Great to store on pantry shelves, great for whipping, can be used as cream, but keep in mind evaporated skim milk has twice as many calories as regular skim milk.

Do not use whipped toppings and imitation sour creams. They are very high in saturated fats and additives.

B.   **YOGURT**

It is almost impossible to buy skim milk yogurt so make your own if you can. A recipe will be found under Basic Recipes. The next best choice is low-fat, unsweetened plain yogurt. You can add your own fruit, if you wish. Commercial sweetened, fruit-flavored yogurt, no matter how natural they say it is, contains about 250 calories. Some of our three course lunches have no more calories than the same 250 and they are far more nutritious and satisfying.

Use low-fat plain yogurt as a substitute for sour cream in dressings, salads, soups and some main dishes. Combined with herbs and seasonings, you will find it is used frequently in our cuisine. One cup of home-made yogurt has 100 calories, a little more than a glass of skim milk. Sour cream runs about 495 calories a cup.

C.   **CHEESE**

Use low-fat (about ½ to 1% fat content) cottage cheese, farmer cheese, whey or hoop cheese. Whey cheese has no salt added. Cottage and farmer cheeses are also available with no added salt.

Avoid cream cheese, cheese spreads and hard cheeses. Swiss, cheddar, mozzarella, American, etc. are all high in fat and salt. One ounce of almost all hard cheeses (one thin slice) runs about 100 calories.

Part-skim cheeses: Many people are misinformed and believe that partially skimmed cheeses are low in fat and calories. Not so . . . Some have as much as 35-40% fat. Some of the low-fat cheeses and imitation cheeses are full of additives and substitutes.

Low cholesterol cheeses have oil substituted for the saturated fat in the milk.

They do have little cholesterol, BUT they have as many fat calories as regular cheese. In addition, many of these also have additives that may be harmful. Have a smaller amount of real cheese.

II. MEAT, FISH, POULTRY AND EGGS — approximately 6 ounces daily

A. **MEAT**

Confine your meat choices to veal, poultry and fish. Eat lean beef occasionally.

Avoid organ meats such as liver, heart, kidney and tongue. They are very high in cholesterol. However, liver may be eaten once in awhile for its iron content.

Avoid all cured, smoked and corned meats, such as bacon, pastrami, sausages and ham. They are all high in both fat and salt and contain harmful additives.

B. **FISH**

Use the low-fat fishes: flounder, haddock, ocean perch and swordifish.

Shellfish, while low in calories are high in cholesterol, shrimp having the highest cholesterol content.

Use water-pack canned fish.

C. **EGGS**

Egg yolks are high in cholesterol. Limit whole eggs to two-three per week.

Egg whites can be used for pancakes, French toast, souffles, crepes and some cakes and breads.

III. BREADS AND CEREALS — 4 or more selections each day

A. **HOT CEREALS:** Oatmeal, Wheatena, and other whole wheat varieties are a wonderful way to start a day, summer and winter. They afford you the best in fiber and nourishment, and are filling as well. Do not use the instant varieties; they are high in salt and digest too quickly.

B. **COLD CEREALS:** Select only from those that have no sugar added, as Grapenuts, puffed wheat, shredded wheat. Some cold cereals are high in sodium, e.g. corn flakes.

C. **WHOLE GRAINS:** Select from brown rice, buckwheat (kasha), barley and bulgar wheat.

D. **BREADS AND CRACKERS:** Select from whole grain breads and crackers, made without sugar or fat. You can also include matzoh, rice cakes, pita bread, sourdough bread, rolls, flatbreads and wheatcrisps.

E. **FLOUR:** Use whole grain flours. White flours should be enriched. Do not use bleached flour. The agents used for bleaching may be harmful (carcionogenic).

    F.   **PASTA:** Use whole grain or vegetable pastas, with no additives.

IV. FRUITS AND VEGETABLES — 4 or more selections

    A.   **FRUIT**

One citrus fruit daily or 4 oz. of orange or grapefruit juice will provide you with an adequate amount of Vitamin C.

Two additional fruits daily for vitamins, minerals and fiber.

Do not substitute canned sweetened fruit for fresh fruit. Half a cup of canned peaches in syrup has 200 calories. One fresh peach has 58 calories. There are fruits packed in their own juice or water-pac available.

Melon in season is great. Cantaloupe and honeydew are low in calories. Remember your portion control. One quarter of an average size cantaloupe has about 40 calories.

Bananas are an excellent source of potassium, are easily digested and lower in calories than you think. They contain about 100 calories for a medium size banana and should be part of your fruit selection every week.

    B.   **VEGETABLES**

Dark green leafy, or dark yellow to orange vegetables should be eaten daily. They include broccoli, spinach, outer green leaves of lettuce, carrots, sweet potatoes, winter squash.

Use several white potatoes per week. They are high in nutrients and fiber. One small potato (about ¼ lb.) has only 70 calories. Skip the butter and sour cream and you have saved 160 calories.

Round out your selections with additional vegetables for their nutritional value, vitamins, minerals and fiber: cabbage, green pepper, mushrooms, tomatoes, cauliflower, zucchini, watercress and cucumbers.

V. DRIED PEAS, BEANS AND LENTILS

An excellent substitute for poultry, fish or meat *but* only when combined with a whole grain to make a complete protein, such as rice or pasta. This source of protein is highly caloric and should be eaten in small quantities.

VI. FATS AND OILS — 1 tablespoon per day

Use in very small quantities. No more than 1 tablespoon daily . . . and that must include cooking and spreading.

Butter, whipped and unsalted — contains saturated fat and cholesterol — must be limited.

Margarine, whipped and unsalted. Check the label for *highest* amount of unsaturated fat, NO salt content and NO additives (almost impossible to find).

Lard, creamed substitutes and canned shortenings: Don't buy them and don't use them.

All of the *polyunsaturated oils* should be used sparingly. Keep in mind that **1** tablespoon equals 120 calories.

fourteen day plan

The Fourteen Day Plan is low in what we like to call the "baddies" — fat, sugar, salt, cholesterol. We have eliminated none of them, just drastically reduced them all, along with the calories. We have given you portion and calorie values in the menus to get you started. After the first few weeks, it is our belief that you will not need to count anything except the pounds and inches you have lost. We know that cutting down fats and sugars, controlling portions and following a pattern of exercise will work. We have husbands, friends, and Spa patrons at Gurney's to prove it.

We know that you can have broiled fish, with boiled or steamed broccoli and a baked potato as a low calorie meal. We want you to have the same low calories with just a little more fuss, and a lot of nutritionally sound delicious and interesting meals that will not bore you out of your diet.

Our daily menus total about 1000 calories. This is based on exact weights and measurements. After the Fourteen Days, increase your calories to about 1200 by adding fruit, a slice of bread or equivalents of other recommended foods in our cuisine.

Our book is addressed to men as well as women. There is no sex discrimination among the overweight. In order to afford men the additional energy needed for their activities, 1500 calories are suggested as a daily intake.

Our food preparation methods are clear and simple. Easy to read directions make cooking a joy and a pleasure. To totally benefit from our Fourteen Day Diet Plan, follow these suggestions and read the explanations:

1. Use a professional stainless steel pan or a coated heavy-bottomed non-stick pan to saute or fry. Some people may prefer not to use a coated pan because of the possible chemical content of the coating.

2. Steaming means placing a basket or colander in a small amount of boiling water, covering and cooking for the shortest possible time to retain color, crispness, vitamins and minerals. This method is used primarily for vegetables.

3. Prepare meat and poultry dishes, as well as soups and stews, enough in advance to allow for firm chilling, so you will be able to skim off fat.

4. When using any ground meat for casseroles, sauces, stews, even meatballs, first lightly cook meat until all pink is gone. Remove to colander to drain off fat. This process is called rendering.

5. Cornstarch, arrowroot and flour can be used and interchanged for thickening agents. Place in jar with liquid being used. Cover tightly, shake vigorously and then add slowly to food, stirring constantly.

6. Remove all visible fat from meat and poultry before cooking. Remove skin from poultry before and/or after cooking.

7. Experiment with herbs and spices. Be brave! Give up that salt shaker and include such pantry shelf spices as curry, cumin, coriander, tarragon, dill and chili. See our chart.

8. Seasonings and spices should never dominate taste. The natural flavor of foods should come through. Use approximately ½ teaspoon of dried herbs or spices, or if using fresh, use 1 tablespoon.

9. NEVER use bouillon cubes or packets that contain salt. Be cautious with soy sauce, catsup, chili sauce, steak sauces and other prepared sauces. They are high in salt, sugar and other additives. There are salt-free bouillons or stocks on the shelves. Check your health food stores. Do not use products with potassium chloride as a substitute for salt.

10. Use natural wines for cooking rather than grocery shelf cooking wines. The cooking wines contain salt and other additives.

11. For soups and stews requiring beans, overnight soaking is often just not enough. Cover beans with water, bring to a quick boil, remove from heat and then allow to soak overnight. This cuts cooking time down by hours.

12. To thicken soups, reduce liquids by long, slow, uncovered simmering or remove vegetables and put through a blender before returning to soup. A potato, cut up and cooked down to mush in the soup also acts as a natural thickening.

13. Lettuce leaves should be torn to reduce browning. Do not cut out the core, but do invert the head of lettuce, slam it down on a flat surface and twist out the core. Store in vegetable keeper wrapped in paper towels, not plastic to retard rusting. Save the dark outer leaves, put them in a plastic bag in your freezer to reserve along with celery tops and bottoms for inclusion in soups. Also, use broccoli stems and asparagus bottoms for the same purpose.

14. Use lemon or vinegar to pick up the flavor of bland vegetables and salads.

15. Use unflavored gelatin for molds, never flavored "jello."

16. Use fruit juices for sweetening and flavor over fresh fruits.

17. Use only fruits canned in their own juices if fresh fruit is not available.

18. Use brown rice as an extender for stuffing pepper, cabbage and meat loaves.

19. Use water pack canned fishes, or drain and wash away all oil.

20. Use lots of vegetables in meat and fish combinations as extenders.

21. Use evaporated skim milk, whipped with an equal amount of whipped sweet butter as a butter extender.

22. Never use fat drippings for gravy.

23. Never add salt to cooking water for vegetables, pasta, rice, etc.

24. If you are on a restricted salt diet, all your foods must be fresh or frozen without salt and no canned food, except salt-free cans, should be used.

25. If you are on a cholesterol restricted diet, eliminate all whole eggs, use egg whites — 2 eggs whites equal 1 whole egg. Use margarine instead of butter.

additional hints and notes

• Vinegar brought to a boil in a new pan will prevent foods from sticking in the future.

• Turn a colander upside down over frying foods; this allows steam to escape and prevents splattering. Do not use a plastic colander.

• If muffins stick to pan, place the pan on a wet towel. The muffins should slide out in a few minutes.

• Toss freshly cut fruit with a little lemon juice to prevent darkening.

• Honey can be easily removed from a measuring cup if you will lightly oil the cup first, then *rinse* out with very hot water.

• Eggs should be used at room temperature for best results.

• Do not add salt to cooking water for any vegetables, especially corn, which will toughen with the addition of salt.

• Thaw frozen fish in a small amount of skim milk. Milk draws out the frozen taste.

• If honey has sugared in the jar, don't throw it away; place jar in a pot of warm water; the sugaring will dissolve.

• Parsley and other fresh herbs from your garden can be stored in a plastic bag or container. For short term, they can be kept crisp in a jar in the refrigerator.

• Keep popcorn around for late snacks, do not top with butter or salt. It's quite tasty and satisfying in its natural state.

• Lemons can be warmed in hot water to produce more juice.

• Fish and meat should be thoroughly drained and dried before cooking.

• Freeze overripe bananas. Save them to use in baking breads or cakes.

• To be sure your gelatin mold will slip out easily, rinse mold pan in cold water and then place in freezer for a few minutes before filling.

• Fresh everything is preferred, but if you must use frozen or canned, be sure to check the salt content.

• Score means to run fork tines down a vegetable, like cucumber or zucchini, to create shallow ruts that make the slices attractive.

• Pare is the same as peel.

• Render means to cook meat slowly to remove fat, mostly in ground meats.

• Saute means to fry in a small amount of oil; for our purposes, we only fry in a very small amount of oil.

• Simmer means to keep cooking food at a low bubble, not to the boiling point.

• Sweat is like simmer, for onions, peppers and other vegetables. Just add a small amount of water, cook over medium heat in a tightly-covered pot.

FOURTEEN DAY PLAN
DAY I

Calories		Portions
	BREAKFAST — *215 Calories*	
40	Grapefruit	½ medium
175	Belgian Apple Toast	1 sandwich
	LUNCH — *215 Calories*	
40	Asparagus Soup Garni	6. oz. serving
65	French Salmon Mousse	⅔ cup
15	Green Salad Bed	Bowl
55	Fresh Pineapple Marron	1 thin slice
40	Whole Wheat Bread	1 very thin slice
	DINNER — *385 Calories*	
40	Greek Avgolemeno Soup (lemon soup)	6 oz. serving
220	Moussaka (eggplant and meat)	1/6th
40	Greek Salad	1 bowl
85	Brandied Pears	½ pear
90	Skim Milk	One 8 oz. glass
905	Calories for the Day	

BELGIAN CINNAMON APPLE TOAST

(serves 4)

8 slices very thin sliced whole wheat bread
½ cup low fat cottage cheese
1 tsp. sugar
¼ tsp. cinnamon for cheese
¼ tsp. cinnamon for apples
2 sweet apples, unpeeled, thinly sliced
1 tsp. lemon juice

1 Tbsp. water
2 lightly beaten egg whites
½ cup fat-free skim milk
1 Tbsp. oil

1. Mix cheese, sugar, cinnamon
2. Toss apples with cinnamon, and lemon juice.
3. Simmer apples in 1 Tbsp. water until just tender.
4. Spread one half cheese mixture over 4 slices of bread.
5. Divide apples over cheese.
6. Cover with remaining cheese.
7. Place remaining slice of bread on top. Press lightly to seal sandwich.
8. Combine eggs and milk, and beat together.
9. Soak sandwiches in milk mixture until all has been absorbed.
10. Heat pan until a drop of water sizzles.
11. Add about half of the oil. Heat again.
12. Fry until golden brown on both sides, using remaining oil if needed. Cover to keep steamy and fluffy. Serve immediately.

175 Calories per sandwich

ASPARAGUS SOUP GARNI

(serves 8)

4 cups stock
1 cup of liquid from asparagus
1 medium onion, sliced
1 medium potato, thinly sliced
1/8 tsp. black pepper
½ tsp. crushed rosemary
1 Tbsp. fresh parsley, chopped
2 14-oz. cans asparagus or 1½ pounds fresh or frozen
Croutons (see BASIC RECIPES)

1. Combine all ingredients except asparagus. Simmer about 15 minutes or until onion and potato are tender.
2. Add asparagus, reserving a few tips for garnish. Simmer 5 minutes more. For fresh or frozen asparagus, cook 10 minutes more.
3. Cool.
4. Puree in blender.
5. Simmer for 5 minutes.
6. When ready to serve, add reserved asparagus tips to each bowl.
7. Garnish with Croutons.

40 calories with croutons for 1/8th recipe.

SALMON MOUSSE

(serves 6)

1 pound can red salmon
1 Tbsp. unflavored gelatin (1 packet)
½ cold water
¼ tsp. paprika
1 tsp. dill weed
½ tsp. garlic powder
¼ tsp. black pepper
1 Tbsp. fresh parsley, chopped
1 tsp. finely minced onion
1 cup low fat plain yogurt
1 Tbsp. lemon juice

Garnishes: cherry tomatoes
    radishes
    green peppers
    lemon, lime
    parsley

1. Skin, bone, drain and mash salmon. Set aside.
2. Sprinkle gelatin over ½ cup of cold water. Heat until gelatin is dissolved, stirring constantly.
3. Combine all ingredients and add to salmon.
4. Rinse 1-quart mold in ice water.
5. Pour salmon mixture into chilled mold.
6. Refrigerate for at least 4 hours.
7. Unmold and serve on a bed of greens. Garnish with cherry tomatoes, radishes, parsley, lemons, strips of green pepper, etc.

65 Calories for 1/12th (approx. ⅔ cup)

This not only makes a good lunch but a wonderful appetizer.

GREEK AVGOLEMENO SOUP
(Lemon Soup)

(serves 6)

½ cup cooked brown rice
5 cups chicken soup (not stock)
1/8 tsp. black pepper
2 egg whites, lightly whisked
1½ tsp. lemon juice
6 paper-thin lemon slices
1 Tbsp. parsley, chopped

1. Heat soup to boiling and add cooked rice. Allow to simmer for 5 minutes.
2. Blend whisked egg whites and lemon juice.
3. Take ½ cup HOT soup and add to lemon-egg mixture VERY slowly, stirring constantly to prevent curdling.
  Add to simmering soup, stirring constantly. Do not boil.
4. Add lemon slices and parsley for garnish.

40 Calories for 6 oz. serving

MOUSSAKA
(Eggplant and Meat)

(serves 6)

1 large eggplant
2 Tbsp. skim milk
4 Tbsp. seasoned bread crumbs
1 large onion, finely chopped
2 clove garlic, finely minced
2 Tbsp. stock or water
½ pound ground veal, very lean
½ cup tomato paste
½ cup tomato sauce
½ cup cold water
½ cup red wine
1 cup mushrooms, sliced
⅓ cup fresh parsley, minced
¼ tsp. each: paprika
           black pepper
           cinnamon
           oregano

1. Wash unpeeled eggplant and slice into ¼ inch slices.
2. Dip in skim milk.
3. Coat lightly in bread crumbs.
4. Bake in preheated 400° oven for 40 minutes.
5. Remove from pan and set aside.
6. Simmer onion and garlic in stock or water until soft and transparent.
7. Render fat out of veal by placing in heavy pan on low heat until all pink is gone. Drain off fat in colander. Add meat to onion and garlic mixture.
8. Add all ingredients and seasonings to meat mixture.
9. Simmer for 10 minutes, stirring occasionally.

Bechamel Sauce for Moussaka

4 Tbsp. unbleached flour
2 cups skim milk
1/8 tsp. black pepper
2 slightly beaten egg whites

1. Shake flour, milk and pepper together in large, tightly covered jar until well blended.
2. Pour into sauce pan and heat slowly, stirring constantly until thickened.
3. Add egg whites very slowly to sauce and stir briskly until sauce is thick and creamy.

Assemblage

Large oblong baking pan
¼ cup Parmesan cheese
Dash fresh ground black pepper

1. Alternate a thin layer of the meat mixture and eggplant starting and ending with the meat mixture.
2. Drizzle Bechamel sauce over entire dish. Insert knife to be sure it gets down into the pan.
3. Sprinkle with the Parmesan cheese and pepper. Bake in preheated 350° oven for 40 minutes.

220 Calories for 1/6th recipe

Do you realize that you're saving about *300* calories per portion by not using oil for frying the eggplant, not using munster cheese and not using butter in the sauce? This has proven to be one of our most popular recipes.

GREEK SALAD

(serves 6)

6 red onion rings
1 head of salad greens
   (1 pound)
2 ripe tomatoes
3 red radishes
1 cucumber
½ green pepper
1 Tbsp. parsley, chopped
¼ pound low fat Farmer cheese
2 black olives, chopped

1. Prepare vegetables for salad.
2. Toss in large bowl, or arrange carefully on large flat platter.
3. Cut or crumble cheese and distribute over salad.
4. Pour dressing over salad and allow to marinate for 15 minutes before serving (see SALAD DRESSINGS).
5. Garnish with the chopped black olives.

40 Calories for salad bowl

BRANDIED PEARS
Top of the stove method

(serves 6)

3 large ripe pears, cut in half
¼ cup cherry wine or brandy
3 grapes or ½ purple plum for each pear half
2 Tbsp. cold water

1. Cut, core, but do not peel pears.
2. Reserve grapes for garnish
3. Place pears in skillet with the water. Spoon liquor over pear halves.
4. Cover and allow to simmer 30 minutes or until pears are tender.
5. Serve warm with grape or plum garnish.

85 Calories for each ½ pear.

DAY II

Calories		Portions
	BREAKFAST — 195 Calories	
40.	Cantaloupe	¼ small
155	Egg in a Basket	1 egg
		1 slice bread
	LUNCH — 265 Calories	
50	Broccoli Soup	6. oz. serving
175	Molded Waldorf Salad with Cottage Cheese	1/6th recipe
40	Rice Cake	1
	DINNER — 420 Calories	
25	Spiced Tomato Juice	½ cup
35	Haitian Vegetable Salad	1 bowl
210	Roulade of Chicken (Chicken with Spinach Stuffing)	1/6th recipe
75	Parslied New Potatoes	1/6th recipe
25	Green Beans with Sage	¾ cup
50	Rhubarb and Strawberries	1/6th recipe
90	Skim Milk	1 glass
970	Calories for the Day	

EGG IN A BASKET

(serves 1)

1 egg
1 slice whole wheat bread (very thin)
1 tsp. butter or margarine

1. Boil water. Gently lower egg into water and poach it for 3 minutes.
2. Toast bread. Cut out center circle. Lay egg into center of buttered bread and top with bread circle.

155 Calories per serving.

BROCCOLI SOUP

(serves 6)

1 medium onion, chopped
1 medium potato, thinly sliced
4 cups chicken or vegetable stock
1 pound broccoli with stalks, reserving 6
    small flowerettes for garnish
1 stalk celery, sliced
1 Tbsp. fresh parsley, chopped
1/8 tsp. black pepper
½ tsp. dried tarragon
6 flowerettes of broccoli for garnish

1. Combine all ingredients in a heavy pot and cook covered for about 30 minutes or until all vegetables are tender.
2. Cool. Puree in a blender. Return to saucepan and simmer 5 minutes more.
3. Add flowerettes to soup and simmer 5 minutes. Serve hot.

50 Calories for 6 oz. serving

MOLDED WALDORF SALAD
with COTTAGE CHEESE

(serves 6)

2 cups pineapple cubes, canned in its own
    juice. Reserve juice.
3 apples cut up into bite-size pieces
3 celery stalks, chopped
¼ cup walnuts, chopped
1 Tbsp. gelatin
Pineapple juice from can.

1 8" ring mold

½ cup low fat cottage cheese

1. Combine all cut-up fruit and nuts in a bowl.
2. Sprinkle gelatin over reserved pineapple juice. Heat until gelatin is dissolved, stirring constantly. Add to fruit.
3. Rinse mold with ice cold water. Pour mixed fruit into mold. Refrigerate until jelled.
4. Unmold salad on a bed of lettuce. Place cottage cheese in center.

175 Calories per serving

HAITIAN VEGETABLE SALAD

(serves 6)

1 cup cooked beets, sliced and drained.
1 cup cooked string beans, sliced and
    drained
1 tomato cut into small cubes
2 small raw zucchini, unpeeled and sliced
    very thin
½ dozen red radishes, sliced very thin
1 cup vinaigrette dressing
    (see SALAD DRESSINGS)

1. Combine all vegetables.
2. Marinate vegetables in dressing for at least 2 hours before serving.

35 Calories for 1/6th recipe.

NICK AND JOYCE MONTE'S FAVORITE: ROULADE DE POULET
(Stuffed Breast of Chicken Roll)

(serves 6)

Stuffing
⅓ cup onion
2 Tbsp. fresh parsley, minced
½ cup chicken stock
1 10-oz. package chopped frozen spinach
¼ tsp. nutmeg
½ cup plain breadcrumbs
1 egg white

1⅓ pounds chicken breast fillets (six pieces)

1. Simmer onions and parsley in stock until soft.
2. Cook spinach and drain well. Add breadcrumbs, seasonings and egg white. Mix well. Add simmered onions and parsley.
3. Pound the fillets until they are about 1/8-inch thick. Lay one next to another overlapping each other along the edges. You will have a piece about 10" long and 8" wide. They will stick together to form an oblong.
4. Spread the spinach mixture over the chicken and roll jelly-roll style. Moisten the edges with a little water or stock to seal.

Sauce
½ cup chicken stock
½ cup dry white wine
2 onions, sliced in rings
½ tsp. dried tarragon
1 tsp. basil

1. Simmer stock, wine, onion and spices together for 3 minutes.
2. Place half the sauce in the pan and cover with one-half of the onion rings.

Assemblage
1. Place chicken roll on top of onions. Pour remainder of sauce over chicken and cover with remaining onion rings. Bake in preheated 350° oven for 45 minutes. Baste frequently.
2. Place under broiler for 2-3 minutes before serving to brown the top.

210 Calories for 1/6 recipe

PARSLIED NEW POTATOES

(serves 6)

6 small new potatoes, equalling about 1 pound
1 Tbsp. butter or margarine
2 Tbsp. chopped parsley

1. Cook potatoes until tender.
2. Slice in thirds and toss with butter and parsley. Serve hot.

75 Calories for one potato

STRING BEANS WITH SAGE

(serves 6)

1 pound fresh string beans
½ tsp. sage

1. Snip ends of beans and leave whole. Steam ten minutes. Do not overcook; they shoud be crunchy. Toss with sage and serve hot.

25 Calories per serving.

RHUBARB AND STRAWBERRIES

(serves 6)

½ pound rhubarb
1 cup strawberries
¼ cup raisins
1 Tbsp. honey
½ cup water

1. Place all ingredients in a saucepan.
2. Cover and simmer 45 minutes or until very soft. Stir frequently.
3. Serve warm.

50 Calories per serving

DAY III

Calories		Portions
	BREAKFAST—240 Calories	
80	Orange	1 medium
100	Wheatena Cereal	¾ cup cooked
40	Whole Wheat Bread	1 slice, very thin
20	Jelly	1 tsp.
	LUNCH—320 Calories	
265	Abruzzi Manicotti with Sauce	2 rolls
15	Tossed Green Salad with Dressing	1 bowl
40	Fresh Peach	1 small
	DINNER—405 Calories	
45	Zucchini Courge Soup	6 oz. serving
190	Coq Farci Asparagus	2 rolls
65	Pomme Provencale	½ cup
20	Cucumber Yogurt Salad	1 bowl
85	Melange of Fresh Fruit	1/6th recipe
90	Skim Milk	1 8 oz. glass
1055	Calories for the Day	

ABRUZZI MANICOTTI

(serves 6)

12 large *uncooked manicotti*

Stuffing
16 oz. low-fat cottage cheese
2 Tbsp. fresh parsley, chopped
2 egg whites, not beaten
2 Tbsp. seasoned bread crumbs
1/8 tsp. black pepper

Sauce
2 small onions, chopped
1 green pepper, chopped
1 cup stock or water for simmering
2 cups mushrooms, sliced
1 28-oz. can mashed tomatoes with juice
½ tsp. dried sweet basil or 1 Tbsp. fresh
  basil, chopped
½ tsp. oregano
1/8 tsp. black pepper
½ tsp. garlic powder
2 Tbsp. red wine vinegar
1 tsp. sugar

1. Combine all ingredients for stuffing and mix until well blended.
2. Using a kitchen knife, stuff raw, uncooked manicotti shells with cheese. Be sure to divide mixture into 12 equal portions.

1. Simmer onions and green pepper in stock.
2. Add mushrooms and simmer 2 minutes
3. Add tomatoes and all seasonings
4. Simmer slowly for 30 minutes in covered saucepan, stirring frequently.
5. Spoon small amount of sauce in bottom of a large oblong pan. Place manicotti in pan.
6. Cover each manicotti with sauce. A little sauce may be reserved for anyone requesting additional sauce when serving. Cover pan tightly with foil.
7. Bake in preheated 350° oven for 40 minutes. Do not peek; steam is needed for proper cooking.
   Serve immediately.

265 Calories for 2 manicotti with sauce

ZUCCHINI COURGE SOUP

(serves 6)

4 cups chicken stock
1 medium onion, chopped
1 medium potato, thinly sliced
1 pound zucchini, thinly sliced
2 Tbsp. fresh parsley, chopped
1/8 tsp. black pepper
½ tsp. rosemary
Pimento for garnish

1. Place all ingredients in stock pot.
2. Cook for 20 minutes or until potato is tender. Cool and puree in blender.
3. Return to flame and simmer 5 minutes.
4. Garnish with thin strips of pimento. Serve steaming hot.

45 Calories for 6 oz. serving.

COQ FARCI ASPARAGUS

(serves 6)

1½ pounds boneless chicken breasts
12 stalks of cooked asparagus
1 egg white, whisked
½ cup seasoned bread crumbs
1 Tbsp. corn oil

1. Trim all fat and gristle from boneless chicken breasts. Slice into 12 portions. Pound as thin as possible.
2. Place one stalk of asparagus in the center of each fillet.

Sauce

½ cup chicken stock
Juice of one small lemon
12 thin lemon slices
4 Tbsp. fresh parsley, chopped
1/8 tsp. fresh black pepper
Cherry tomatoes for garnish
Fresh parsley for garnish

3. Roll each fillet to enclose asparagus. Do not attempt to tuck ends. Chicken will seal itself in the cooking.
4. Dip each roll in whisked egg white and then into bread crumbs.
5. Heat pan until a drop of water sizzles. Add half the oil and heat again.
6. Fry each roll to golden brown on both sides, only using as much of the remaining oil as needed.
7. Set aside in serving casserole. Arrange attractively in pan.

1. Combine all sauce ingredients in small saucepan.
2. Simmer 2 minutes.
3. Pour or spoon sauce over each chicken roll. Place lemon slice atop each.
4. Cover tightly and bake in preheated 350° oven for 30 minutes. Baste and serve. Garnish with cherry tomatoes and parsley.

190 Calories for 2 rolls

POMME PROVENCALE

(serves 6)

3 medium potatoes, peeled and sliced ½" thick
¼ pound mushrooms, sliced
1 onion, sliced into rings
1 pound can plum tomatoes cut into quarters
¼ tsp. black pepper
¼ tsp. garlic powder
1 bay leaf
1 cup liquid from can of tomatoes, or water

3 quart oven casserole with cover

1. Combine all ingredients in large bowl. Mix together so that potatoes will absorb all seasonings. Arrange in casserole.
2. Bake in tightly covered casserole in preheated 350° oven for 1 hour.
3. Bake 10 additional minutes uncovered for crusty top, if desired.

65 Calories for 1/6th recipe.

CUCUMBER SALAD WITH YOGURT DRESSING

(serves 6)

3 cucumbers, peeled

Dressing
½ cup low fat plain yogurt
½ cup chives, minced (fresh if possible)
¼ tsp. garlic powder
2 tsp. fresh parsley, chopped
1/8 tsp. dry dill weed
1 tsp. prepared mustard
1 tsp. onion, minced

1. Wash cucumbers and slice very thin. Place in large, attractive salad bowl.
2. Combine all dressing ingredients.
3. Mix, beat or shake until blended.
4. Pour over cucumbers and toss. Refrigerate for at least 2 hours before serving.

20 Calories per serving

MELANGE OF FRESH FRUIT

(serves 6)

Combine 6 different kinds of fresh fruits: apple, orange, half melon, pear, peach etc.

Garnish with berries in season.
Chill in stemmed glasses.

85 Calories for 1/6th recipe.

DAY IV

Calories		Portions
	BREAKFAST—175 Calories	
40	Grapefruit	½ medium
110	Southern Buttermilk Pancakes	3 pancakes
25	Hot Strawberry-Pineapple Sauce	2 Tbsp.
	LUNCH—300 Calories	
25	Spiked Tomato Juice	4 oz. serving
195	Chef's Salad	Large bowl
80	Baked Stuffed Apple	1 small
	DINNER—395 Calories	
130	Yellow Split Pea Soup	6 oz. serving
135	Mushroom Stuffed Fish Rolls	2 rolls
35	String Beans with Pearled Onions	1/6th recipe
15	Tossed Green Salad	1 bowl
80	Banana-Grape Medley	1/8th recipe
90	Skim Milk	One 8 oz. glass
960	Calories for the day.	

SOUTHERN BUTTERMILK PANCAKES

(serves 6)

1 cup whole wheat pancake mix
1 cup low fat buttermilk
1 whole egg
1 tsp. corn oil

1. Mix buttermilk and egg together.
2. Add to pancake mix. Batter will be lumpy.
3. Heat pan until a drop of water sizzles. Rub pan with a pastry brush with some part of the 1 tsp. of oil. Heat again.
4. Pour in about ⅓ cup of the batter. This will make a portion of 3 pancakes, 3 inches in size.

Sauce—Strawberry-Pineapple

1 cup fresh strawberries, or no-sugar frozen pack strawberries
1 cup pineapple in its own juice
1 Tbsp. lemon juice

1. Place ingredients in blender. Whip until smooth.
2. Heat slowly in small saucepan.
3. Serve hot over pancakes, using 2 Tbsp. for each 3 pancake portion.

110 Calories for 3 pancakes
25 Calories for 2 Tbsp. sauce

SPIKED TOMATO JUICE

(serves 1)

4 oz. tomato juice
¼ tsp. horseradish
½ tsp. lime juice

1. Chill tomato juice
2. Add horseradish and lime juice

25 Calories per serving

CHEF'S SALAD

(serves 1)

¼ cup (2 oz.) low fat farmer cheese
2 oz. white meat turkey
¼ head lettuce greens
2 scallions
½ tomato
6 slices cucumber
¼ green pepper
4 red radishes
1 small carrot
1 stalk celery

½ cup salad dressing of your choice

1. Cut cheese into cubes or crumble.
2. Slice turkey into thin strips.
3. Prepare salad vegetables as desired.
4. Toss salad in large bowl.
5. Pour dressing over and toss again.
6. Arrange cheese and turkey strips atop green salad.
7. Allow to stand 5 to 10 minutes for dressing to be absorbed into salad.

195 Calories each salad bowl

BAKED STUFFED APPLES

(1 apple each serving)

1 small baking apple, washed
1 tsp. white raisins
1/8 tsp. cinnamon
1 tsp. lemon juice

¼ cup cold water

1. Slice off top of apple and set top aside.
2. Core and pit the apple.
3. Insert raisins and lemon juice in cavity.
4. Sprinkle cinnamon on apple and place top back on apple.
5. Arrange in baking pan and pour cold water on bottom.
6. Bake in preheated 350° oven for 1 hour. Test for firmness desired. May require longer baking if a soft apple is desired.

80 Calories each apple

YELLOW SPLIT PEA SOUP

(serves 6)

1 cup yellow split peas
1 large marrow bone (optional)
2 carrots, dices
2 large onions, chopped (about 1½ cups)
2 stalks of celery with leaves, sliced
Cold water to equal 1½ quarts
½ tsp. marjoram
½ tsp. thyme
¼ tsp. black pepper
Fresh parsley for garnish

1. Place split peas in large soup kettle. Cover with water and bring to a boil.
2. Remove from heat and allow to soak overnight.
   Note: Some split peas and bean are presoaked. We soak all our peas and bean overnight.
3. Add marrow bone.
4. Add aditional water, seasonings and all vegetables. Cover and stir frequently while cooking.
5. Cook for 2 hours or until all split peas are softened. Keep at low boil.
6. Garnish with fresh sprig of parsley. Serve steaming hot.

130 Calories for 6 oz. serving.
This soup thickens when standing.

MUSHROOM STUFFED FISH ROLLS

(serves 6)

1 onion, finely chopped
¼ pound mushrooms, finely chopped
2 Tbsp. stock or water
1½ pounds thin flounder fillets; should equal 12 small fillets
2 Tbsp. lemon juice
½ tsp. dry dill week or 1 tsp. fresh dill, chopped
1/8 tsp. black pepper
½ cup seasoned bread crumbs
¼ cup dry white wine
Paprika for color
Parsley sprigs and cherry tomatoes and lemon wedges for garnish.

1. Simmer onions and mushrooms in stock until golden brown.
2. Pat dry and set on a paper towel to drain all liquid.
3. Combine lemon juice, dill, pepper and bread crumbs with onion and mushroom mixture. Blend together.
   Divide mixture into 12 equal portions. Place a portion in the center of each fillet.
4. Roll up to enclose stuffing. There is no need to tuck or skewer. Fillets will seal in the baking.
5. Rub large baking pan with oil. Place fillets in pan and spoon wine over them. Then sprinkle each one with a dash of paprika.
6. Bake in preheated 400° oven for 15 minutes or until fish appears flaky and white. Garnish with red cherry tomatoes, green parsley and yellow lemon wedges for a colorful presentation. Serve immediately.

135 Calories for each serving

STRING BEANS WITH PEARLED ONIONS

(serves 6)

1 pound string beans, cut into 2″ pieces
½ pound tiny, white onions, fresh or canned
¼ tsp. dried sage, crushed

1. Steam string beans and onions.
2. If using canned onions, drain and discard liquid, rinse in colander.
3. Sprinkle with sage, last 2 minutes of cooking time.
4. Serve hot.

35 Calories for 1/6th recipe

BANANA-GRAPE MEDLEY

(serves 8)

1 Tbsp. gelatin or 1 packet
½ cup cold water
2 Tbsp. sugar
1 cup orange juice, unsweetened
6 Tbsp. lemon juice
3 small ripe bananas, mashed
1 cup grapes in season, pitted and halved
6 mint leaves

1. Sprinkle gelatin over cold water. Heat until gelatin is dissolved, stirring constantly.
2. Add sugar and mix well.
3. Add orange juice, lemon juice, and mashed banana.
4. Whip with electric mixer. Cool in refrigerator until slightly thickened, which takes about 1 hour.
5. Whip again to frothy consistency.
6. Fold in grapes, reserving several halves for garnish.
7. Spoon into goblets or sherbet glasses.
8. Top with remaining grapes and secure mint leaf along side for garnish. Chill for about 1 hour until set. Serve cold.

80 Calories per serving

DAY V

Calories		Portions
	BREAKFAST — 225 Calories	
75	Orange slices	1 small
150	Peach Crepe	2 crepes
	LUNCH — 240 Calories	
150	Chicken Livers with Apple Rings	1/6th recipe
75	Boiled, Parslied Potato	1 small
15	Tomato and Cucumber Salad	½ tomato and ½ cucumber
	DINNER — 405 Calories	
75	Mushroom Bisque	6 oz. serving
180	Poached Cod with Green Sauce	1/6th recipe
35	Baked Idaho Potato Skins	1 skin, halved
25	Tossed Salad with Dressing	1 bowl
15	Asparagus with Lemon	4 stalks
75	Melon in Season	½ melon, small
90	Skim Milk	One 8 oz. glass
960	Calories for the day.	

PEACH CREPE

(serves 8 — makes 16 crepes)

4 egg whites
1 cup unbleached flour
1¼ cups skim milk
2 tsp. baking powder
1 Tbsp. oil

Clean dishcloth on flat surface

Wax paper for protecting layers

1. Combine all ingredients. Blend into batter with whisk. It should be slightly lumpy.
2. Heat pan until drop of water sizzles. Add 1 tsp. oil. Heat again.
3. Pour ¼ cup or less of batter into well heated pan. Slide batter around to distribute evenly and thinly.
4. Rotate to keep crepe free of pan. When set and firm, slide from pan, done side down, onto clean dishcloth. Continue until all 16 crepes are done, using additional oil as necessary.
5. You can use a layer of waxed paper in between for storing in freezer. Be sure crepes are cool before covering with wax paper. Crepes can be frozen for future use, stuffed or unstuffed.

Filling

3 cups peaches, chopped
½ cup raisins
½ tsp. cinnamon
1 tsp. lemon juice
3 Tbsp. unsweetened orange juice
1 tsp. oil
2 Tbsp. skim milk
¼ tsp. cinnamon combined with ½ tsp. sugar for sprinkling

1. Simmer peaches and seasonings with raisins in small saucepan with the orange juice until peaches are cooked, but firm. Cool. Remove skin from peaches.
2. Divide mixture into the number of crepes you have made.

Assemblage

1. Roll or fold over in thirds. Do not attempt to tuck in ends. Crepe will hold its filling if you are gentle.
2. Oil bottom of baking dish. Arrange crepes so they do not touch in large baking pan.

3. Using a pastry brush, brush crepes with skim milk. Bake in preheated 350° oven for 15 minutes or until heated through. Sprinkle with cinnamon and sugar. Serve hot.

150 Calories for each 2 filled crepes.

CHICKEN LIVERS WITH APPLE RINGS

(serves 6)

2 medium apples
½ tsp. lemon juice
½ cup water
1 tsp. oil
1 pound chicken livers, trimmed
½ pound mushrooms, sliced
1 small onion, sliced into thin rings
¼ tsp. cinnamon
1 tsp. brown sugar
Dash black pepper

1. Core, but do not peel apples. Slice into rings, each apple yielding 6 rings. Sprinkle with lemon juice.
2. Simmer apples in large, flat, frying pan. Remove from pan as soon as they soften. Place in large baking casserole.
3. Heat oil in frying pan.
4. Add onions and saute until just transparent.
5. Add mushrooms and saute for 5 minutes.
6. Add livers and cook until no longer pink. Do not overcook. This should take about 10 minutes.
7. Add seasonings. Toss gently; do not mash livers.
8. Place livers over apples. Heat together in preheated 350° oven for 10 minutes.

140 Calories for each serving combined with apple ring.

PARSLIED BOILED POTATO

(serves 6)

6 small potatoes
½ tsp. dried parsley or 1 Tbsp. fresh parsley, chopped
Dash fresh ground black pepper

1. Peel and cook potatoes until tender, but not mushy.
2. Sprinkle with parsley and black pepper.

75 Calories each potato

TOMATO AND CUCUMBER SALAD

(serves 6)

3 small tomatoes
3 small cucumbers
1 Tbsp. fresh basil, chopped
1 Tbsp. wine vinegar

1. Slice tomatoes and cucumbers.
2. Sprinkle with vinegar and fresh chopped basil.

25 Calories per 1/6th serving

MUSHROOM BISQUE

(serves 6)

3 cups stock
1 medium onion, cut up
1 small potato, thinly sliced
1 cup celery, sliced
10 oz. mushrooms, sliced with stems
1 Tbsp. fresh parsley, chopped
1/8 tsp. black pepper
1 cup skim evaporated milk
1 Tbsp. cornstarch or arrowroot
6 slices of mushroom for garnish

1. Place stock, vegetables and seasonings in soup pot.
2. Simmer for 30 minutes or until potato begins to cook apart. This is your thickening agent. Cool slightly.
3. Add 1 cup skim evaporated milk that has been blended with 1 Tbsp. cornstarch or arrowroot.
4. Puree in blender. Return to soup pot and simmer for 15 minutes or until steaming hot.
5. Serve immediately with a slice of mushroom for garnish.

75 Calories for 6 oz. serving

POACHED COD WITH GREEN SAUCE

(serves 6)

2 pounds cod steaks, cut into 6 portions

Green Sauce
1 cup low fat plain yogurt
⅓ cup green onion or leek, chopped. Use as much of the green as is tender
¼ cup fresh parsley, chopped
Pinch of sage

Pinch of tarragon
Pinch of cayenne pepper
2 Tbsp. lemon juice
1/8 tsp. black pepper

6 thin strips of pimento
Parsley sprigs
6 very thin lemon slices

1. Poach fish in court bouillon (see STOCKS), about 10 minutes. Allow to cool and drain before chilling.
2. Place all ingredients in blender with yogurt. Puree. Chill for 2 hours before serving.

3. Spoon sauce over each fish steak. Reserve additional sauce for requests.
4. Garnish each with pimento strip, sprig of fresh parsley, and thin lemon slice.

180 Calories for each fish steak with sauce

BAKED POTATO SKINS

(serves 1)

1 large Idaho or #1 Russet baking potato

1. Bake potato until tender.
2. Remove from oven; allow to cool slightly and cut in half. Scoop out all potato filling and reserve for future use. It may be frozen.
   Sprinkle skin with black pepper.
3. Place on baking sheet. Return to preheated 350° oven for 20 minutes to crisp the skins.
4. Serve immediately. Keep watch; do not allow to burn.

35 Calories for 2 halves

TOSSED SALAD

(serves 6)

1 head Romaine lettuce or other greens
1 large cucumber, sliced
1 large tomato, cut into wedges
6 radishes, sliced
6 carrot curls

1. Wash and tear lettuce into small pieces. Toss all vegetables with dressing.

25 Calories per serving

DAY VI

Calories		Portions
	BREAKFAST — 220 Calories	
40	Grapefruit	½ medium
120	Shredded Wheat and Skim Milk	¾ cup wheat plus ¼ cup skim milk
40	Whole Wheat Bread	1 very thin slice
20	Jelly	1 tsp.
	LUNCH — 270 Calories	
210	Amagansett Fish Chowder	10 oz.
60	Caesar Salad and Croutons	Bowl
	DINNER — 515 Calories	
60	Antipasto with Mustard Sauce	Bowl
235	Chicken Pizziola	1/6th recipe
95	Pasta	½ cup
30	Broccoli with Lemon	3 stalks
95	Fruit Amoretta	½ cup
90	Skim Milk	One 8 oz. glass
1095	Calories for the day.	

AMAGANSETT FISH CHOWDER

(serves 6)

3 shallots, chopped fine
1 large onion, chopped fine
4 celery stalks with tops, chopped
¼ cup water
¼ cup fresh peas
1 cup carrots, diced and cooked
4 small potatoes, diced
4 cups stock
¼ tsp. black pepper
¼ tsp. thyme

1/8 tsp. sage
½ cup white wine
1 Tbsp. corn starch or arrowroot
¼ cup cold water
1½ pounds codfish, cut into bite-size pieces
1 cup evaporated skim milk
Black pepper for garnish
Parsley for garnish

1. Simmer shallots, onions and celery in water for 10 minutes.
2. Combine all vegetables and seasonings with onion mixture in large pot. Add stock.
   Bring to a low boil and cook for 30 minutes or until potatoes are tender.
3. Reduce heat and continue to simmer.
4. Mix cornstarch into cold water to use as thickening (roux). Add to simmering chowder. Add milk.
   Stir and continue to simmer for 5 minutes.
5. Add fish and stir gently. Do NOT stir again or fish will flake apart. Simmer for 5 minutes.
6. Serve steaming hot garnished with a grind of fresh black pepper and/or a small sprig of fresh parsley.

210 Calories for 10 oz. serving

CAESAR SALAD

(serves 6)

6 slices of red onion rings
3 heads of Romaine lettuce (1½ to 2 pounds total)
1 cup croutons (see BASIC RECIPES)

1. Wash, drain, dry and tear lettuce into serving pieces for salad. Toss with onion rings. Place in large attractive salad bowl.

Caesar Dressing
3 Tbsp. wine vinegar
1 Tbsp. corn oil
6 cloves of garlic, crushed
Juice of one lemon
Dash of Worcesteshire Sauce
1/8 tsp. black pepper

1. Combine all ingredients: vinegar, oil, garlic, lemon juice, Worcesteshire Sauce and black pepper.
2. Shake vigorously in tightly closed jar. Store overnight before using.
3. Pour dressing over salad and allow to marinate for 15 minutes before serving.
4. Garnish with croutons.

60 Calories per serving

ANTIPASTO

(serves 8)

1 small white cauliflower, in flowerettes
1 medium unskinned zucchini, cut in sticks
2 carrots in curls
12 radishes in rosettes
12 stalks of celery, cut in thin sticks
1 pound cherry tomatoes
1 cucumber, unpeeled and sliced

1. Arrange prepared vegetables attractively, alternating colors, on large platter.

Mustard Sauce

1 cup cold water
⅓ cup non-fat dry skim milk powder
1 Tbsp. flour
3 tsp. prepared mustard
¼ tsp. dill seed
1/8th tsp. black pepper
¼ tsp. celery seed

1. Combine all ingredients. Use egg beater to mix together and to be sure flour is not lumping.
2. Pour in saucepan and heat over low flame for 5 minutes or until slightly thickened. Serve warm over Antipasto.

60 Calories for 1/8th recipe

CHICKEN PIZZIOLA

(serves 6)

1 pound chicken cutlets
¼ cup skim milk
6 Tbsp. seasoned bread crumbs
1 Tbsp. corn oil

1. Trim and cut into 12 thin cutlets.
2. Dip cutlets in milk, then lightly coat with bread crumbs.
3. Set aside on paper towel to dry. Heat pan until a drop of water sizzles. Add one half of the oil. Heat again.
4. Brown cutlets on both sides, using as little of remaining 1 Tbsp. of oil as possible.

Sauce

2 cloves of garlic, crushed
2 medium onions, minced
½ cup water for simmering
1 28-oz. can plum tomatoes in puree
1 4-oz. can tomato paste, plus 4 oz. water
1 Tbsp. red wine vinegar
1 tsp. sugar
½ tsp. oregano
½ tsp. sweet basil
¼ tsp. black pepper
¼ tsp. garlic powder

1. Simmer onions and garlic in water until golden brown and tender.
2. Add all ingredients. Cover and cook at low heat for ½ hour. Stir frequently; do NOT allow to boil rapidly.

Cheese Mixture
4 oz. low fat cottage cheese
1 egg white
1/8 tsp. garlic powder
1/8 tsp. black pepper

1 Tbsp. Parmesan cheese for garnish

1. Combine cheese, egg white, garlic powder and black pepper. Chill cheese mixture for 30 minutes to allow it to become firm.

Assemblage

1. Place small amount of sauce on the bottom of large casserole. Arrange cutlets.
2. Place spoonful of cheese misture on top of each cutlet. Cover with sauce. Garnish with parmesan cheese. Bake in a preheated 350° oven for 20 minutes.

235 Calories each two cutlets

AMORETTO DI SARONNO

(serves 6)

1 medium apple, cut into 6 slices
6 slices fresh pineapple, thinly cut
1 orange, cut into 6 slices
2 fresh, ripe peaches, sliced into thirds
3 Tbsp. Amoretto liqueur
6 small mint leaves

1. Start with a thin pineapple slice. Add 1 slice of apple. Top with 1 slice of orange. Add 1 slice peach.
2. Use about ½ Tbsp. liqueur on each fruit plate. Allow fruit to marinate and serve at room temperature. Garnish with mint leaf.

95 Calories per serving

DAY VII

Calories		Portions
	BREAKFAST — 230 Calories	
40	Melon in season	¼ small
190	Muffin Cheese Melt	1 whole wheat English muffin
	LUNCH — 320 Calories	
45	Apple Juice	½ cup
195	Turkey-Asparagus Salad	1/6th recipe
40	Bread Stick	1
40	Boiled Grapefruit	½ medium
	DINNER — 400 Calories	
60	Potato-Leek Soup	6 oz. serving
140	Flounder with Mandarin Oranges	2 fillets
75	Baked Acorn Squash	½ small
30	Brussel Sprouts with Tarragon	⅔ cup
15	Tossed Green Salad	Bowl
80	Peach-Rum Mousse	1/8th recipe
90	Skim Milk	One 8 oz. glass
1040	Calories for the day.	

MUFFIN CHEESE MELT

(serves 1)

1 whole wheat English muffin
4 Tbsp. low fat cottage cheese
¼ tsp. caraway seeds

1. Split muffin with fork and lightly toast.
2. Spread cheese equally over both halves. Sprinkle with caraway seeds.
3. Broil for 2-3 minutes until bubbly. Serve immediately.

190 Calories each muffin

TURKEY-ASPARAGUS SALAD

(serves 6)

18 asparagus stalks
1 pound turkey breast, thinly sliced
6 peach halves, cooked or canned in its
  own juice
Lettuce leaves
1 green pepper cut in strips
1 red pepper cut in strips

1. Cut off tough ends of asparagus and steam until tender. Do not overcook.
2. Roll one slice of turkey around each asparagus stalk. Let ends stick out.
3. Arrange lettuce on a plate. Place peach half in center. Lay turkey roll-ups around plate like spokes of a wheel. Place strips of red and green pepper between turkey roll-ups.

195 Calories per serving

BROILED GRAPEFRUIT

(serves 1)

½ small grapefruit
Dash cinnamon

1. Place ½ sectioned grapefruit under broiler for 4 minutes.
2. Sprinkle with cinnamon.
3. Serve hot.

40 Calories for ½ grapefruit

POTATO-LEEK SOUP

(serves 8)

1 onion, thinly sliced
3 leeks and tops, thinly sliced
1 cup stock
1 pound potatoes, thinly sliced
1 stalk celery, sliced
4 sprigs parsley, chopped
4 cups stock
½ tsp. marjoram
1/8 tsp. white pepper
Minced chives for garnish

1. Simmer onion and leek until golden brown and tender.
2. Using a large stock pot, combine all ingredients and seasonings with simmered onions and leeks. Cook about 20 minutes or until potatoes are tender.
3. Puree in blender. Serve hot with chive garnish.

60 Calories for 6 oz. serving

FLOUNDER STUFFED WITH MANDARIN ORANGES

(serves 6)

1½ pounds fillet of flounder or sole cut into 12 portions

Marinade for fillets
1 Tbsp. corn oil
3 Tbsp. lemon juice
½ tsp. dill weed
½ tsp. curry powder
½ tsp. cumin
1/8 tsp. black pepper

24 Mandarin orange slices for stuffing
Lemon wedges for garnish
Parsley sprigs for garnish

1. Pat fillets dry with paper towels.
2. Marinate fillets about 15 minutes. Turn once to be sure flavor has been absorbed.
3. Pour enough marinade to coat bottom of pan. Spread along bottom and sides.
4. Place 2 orange sections in each fillet. Roll, placing open side down. Fillet will seal itself in the baking.
5. Arrange in baking pan. Pour remaining marinade over fish.
6. Bake in preheated 400° oven for 10-12 minutes until fish appears flaky and snow-white.
7. Serve at once with lemon wedge and parsley sprig for garnish.

140 Calories per serving of 2 fillets

ACORN SQUASH

(serves 6)

3 small acorn squash (about 2 pounds) cut in half
1 Tbsp. honey
1 Tbsp. cold water
Dash of cinnamon

1. Remove and discard squash seeds.
2. Conbine honey with water in small container. Divide mixture equally in all 6 cavities. Sprinkle with cinnamon.
3. Bake in preheated 350° oven for 1 hour. Cover with foil for first 30 minutes.
4. Uncover and bake for an additional 30 minutes, until golden brown and tender. Serve hot. NO butter is needed.

75 Calories for each half

BRUSSEL SPROUTS WITH TARRAGON LEAVES

(serves 6)

1 pound, or 1 quart container
  Brussel Sprouts
¼ tsp. tarragon leaves, dried and crushed

1. Steam Brussel Sprouts to tenderness.
2. Sprinkle with tarragon leaves just before serving.

30 Calories for approximately 4 Brussel Sprouts serving

PEACH-RUM MOUSSE

(serves 8)

1 Tbsp. unflavored gelatin (1 packet)
½ cup water
2½ cups cooked peaches, skinned
2 Tbsp. rum
½ cup ice cold evaporated skim milk
1 Tbsp. sugar

12 strawberries for garnish

1. Sprinkle gelatin over cold water. Heat until gelatin is dissolved, stirring constantly.
2. Add peaches and rum. Puree in blender.
3. Refrigerate until almost set.
4. Whip ice cold evaporated milk until it stands in peaks. Add sugar gradually and continue whipping until all sugar is blended in. Fold into peaches.
5. Place in individual sherbet glasses. Chill several hours to set. Serve cold with strawberry garnish.

80 Calories per serving

DAY VIII

Calories		Portions
	BREAKFAST—250 Calories	
40	Grapefruit	½ medium
125	Oatmeal with Milk	⅓ cup raw oatmeal with ¼ cup skim milk
65	Bagel Thins	2 thins
20	Cottage Cheese	2 Tbsp.
	LUNCH—285 Calories	
210	Curried Chicken with Rice	1/6th recipe
25	String Bean Salad Vinaigrette Dressing	¾ cup
50	Fresh Peach	1 medium
	DINNER—370 Calories	
125	Mussels	10
	Lemon Butter	1 tsp.
15	Green Salad with Dressing	1 bowl
190	Greek Cod Gumbo	1/6th recipe
40	Cantaloupe	¼ small
90	Skim Milk	One 8 oz. glass
995	Calories for the Day	

OATMEAL

(serves 1)

⅓ cup oatmeal
1 cup water

1. Cook according to directions on package.

100 Calories for Oatmeal
25 Calories for milk poured on top

BAGEL THINS

With a very sharp knife slice bagel into six thin circles. Toast. These can be kept for a long time.

65 Calories for two thins.
20 Calories for 2 Tbsp. salt-free cottage cheese, 1% fat.

CURRIED CHICKEN WITH RICE

(serves 6)

1 pound chicken breasts
¼ cup seasoned bread crumbs
2 Tbsp. skim milk
1 Tbsp. oil

2 onions thinly sliced
2 tsp. curry powder
½ tsp. cinnamon
½ tsp. black pepper
1 Tbsp. poppy seeds
1 tsp. ground ginger
Juice of one lemon
½ cup chicken stock

2 cups cooked brown rice
Cherry tomatoes and parsley for garnish.

1. Remove all skin and fat from chicken breasts. Cut into 2" serving pieces. Dip into skim milk, then into bread crumbs.
2. Heat large frying pan until a drop of water sizzles. Add oil and heat again. Pour off excess oil and reserve for second side. Saute chicken on both sides until golden brown. Remove to platter.
3. Place onion rings in still-heating pan and brown. Cover to keep moisture in.
4. Combine chicken stock, onions and seasonings and simmer for 10 minutes in frying pan.
5. Add chicken and simmer 10 minutes longer.
6. Serve chicken over a bed of rice.

130 Calories per serving Curried Chicken
80 Calories per serving brown rice.

GREEN BEAN SALAD

(serves 6)

1 pound green beans
1 cup vinaigrette dressing
   (see SALAD DRESSINGS)

1. Snip ends and cut into 1-inch pieces. Steam until tender, but crisp. Cool.
2. Marinate beans in dressing for at least 2 hours.

25 Calories for ¾ cup

MUSSELS WITH LEMON BUTTER

(serves 6)

5 dozen mussels
1 Tbsp. butter or margarine
3 Tbsp. lemon juice

1. Place mussels in a basket over boiling water. Cover. Steam mussels for about 5 minutes until they open up.
2. Melt butter and add lemon juice. Serve in a warmed cup for dipping.

125 Calories for 10 mussels

GREEK COD GUMBO

(serves 6)

¼ cup stock
1 cup green pepper, chopped
1 cup onion, chopped
1 tsp. garlic, minced
1 16-oz. can tomatoes, chopped
¾ cup stock (fish or chicken)
½ tsp. dried crushed basil
1 Tbsp. fresh parsley, chopped
1/8 tsp. fresh ground black pepper
Dash chili powder
1 10-oz. package frozen okra
6 small cooked potatoes, equalling about 1 pound
1½ pound fish fillets: cod, sole or haddock

1. Simmer onions, green pepper and garlic in stock until transparent.
2. Add tomatoes and stock to onion mixture. Add seasonings and simmer 30 minutes.
3. Cut okra into bite-size pieces. Cut potatoes into ½-inch slices. Add potatoes and okra to tomato mixture and simmer 5 minutes.
4. Cut fish into 1" cubes. Add to simmering mixture and stir immediately while fish is still firm. Do not stir again. Cook 5-6 minutes more until fish is snowy white.
   Serve on heated platter.

190 Calories per serving

DAY IX

Calories		Portions
	BREAKFAST— 230 Calories	
80	Orange	1 medium
150	Blueberry Cottage Cheese Pancakes with Orange Sauce	¼ recipe
	LUNCH— 270 Calories	
80	Vichyssoise	6. oz. serving
110	Armenian Baked Stuffed Eggplant	½ small eggplant
80	Pita Bread-Whole Wheat Sesame	1 4" round
	DINNER— 470 Calories	
70	Gaspacho Andalusian	6 oz. serving
230	Paella Valencia	1/6th recipe
15	Arranged Salad	1/6th recipe
80	French Bread	1½" slice
75	Pineapple-Lemon Whip	1 sherbet glass
90	Skim Milk	One 8 oz. glass
1060	Calories for the day.	

BLUEBERRY COTTAGE CHEESE PANCAKES WITH HONEYED ORANGE SAUCE

(serves 4)

¼ cup skim milk
1 egg
½ cup low fat cottage cheese
½ cup whole wheat pancake mix
½ cup blueberries, unsweetened and drained
1 tsp. oil

1. Mix milk and egg together.

Sauce
1 Tbsp. honey
¼ cup orange juice
1 Tbsp. lemon juice

2. Add cottage cheese and mix well.
3. Add to pancake mix. Do not overbeat.
4. Add blueberries and mix lightly.
5. Heat pan until a drop of water sizzles. Add oil and heat again.
6. Using about one Tbsp. of batter for each pancake, fry on both sides until brown.
7. Mix sauce ingredients together and simmer for 3 minutes. Serve hot with the pancakes.

125 Calories per serving
25 Calories per Tbsp. sauce

VICHYSSOISE

(serves 8)

1 onion, chopped
3 leeks, thinly sliced
1 pound potatoes, peeled and thinly sliced
1 stalk celery, cut up into small pieces
4 sprigs parsley
½ tsp. marjoram
1/8 tsp. white pepper
5 cups chicken or vegetable stock
½ cup skim evaporated milk
Chives for garnish

1. Combine all ingredients in a saucepan and simmer until tender.
2. Cool slightly and then puree in a blender. Return to saucepan, add milk and simmer 5 minutes more.
3. Cool. Chill and serve with minced chives.

80 Calories for 6 oz. serving

ARMENIAN BAKED STUFFED EGGPLANT

(serves 6)

3 small eggplants (about 1 pound each)
2 onions, chopped
3 cloves garlic or ½ tsp. garlic powder
½ cup stock
1 green pepper, chopped
2 cups mushrooms, sliced
¼ cup parsley, chopped
1 tsp. oregano
¼ tsp. fresh ground pepper
¼ tsp. dried basil
½ cup plain breadcrumbs

Topping
¼ tsp. chives
½ cup unflavored breadcrumbs
1 Tbsp. butter or margarine
Dash garlic powder
1 Tbsp. Parmesan cheese

1. Wash eggplant, but do not peel. Cut in half lengthwise. Bake in preheated 400° oven for one hour until tender.
2. Scoop out interior, leaving about ½ rim of eggplant around edge. Finely chop the interior of the eggplant and set aside.
3. Simmer onions and garlic in stock until transparent.
4. Add green pepper, mushrooms and seasonings. Simmer until tender.
5. Combine eggplant, sauteed onions, mushrooms and pepper with the bread-crumbs. Divide into six equal portions and stuff eggplant shells.
6. Melt margarine or butter. Add topping of breadcrumbs and seasonings. Com-bine and spread on eggplant. Sprinkle cheese over bread-crumbs. Bake in preheated 350° oven for 30 minutes.

110 Calories per serving

GAZPACHO ANDALUSIAN

(serves 6)

1 green pepper
1 small onion
1 cucumber, peeled
1 16-oz. can whole tomatoes
2 cups tomato juice (salt-free)
2 cloves garlic, minced, or ½ tsp. garlic
  powder
4 Tbsp. wine vinegar
½ tsp. oregano
½ tsp. dry basil or 2 fresh leaves
½ tsp. dill

Garnish
1 small onion
1 small cucumber
½ green pepper
1 cup shredded wheat bits

1. Wash and cut all vegetables into small pieces, except those for the garnish.
2. Puree vegetables, juice, spices and vinegar in blender.
3. Chill in refrigerator at least 2 hours before serving.
4. Coarsely chop all garnish vegetables. Set out in individual chilled bowls for Gazpacho.

70 Calories for 6 oz. serving

PAELLA VALENCIA

(serves 6)

Sauce
½ cup stock
3 cloves garlic or ½ tsp. garlic powder
1 onion chopped
1 cup chicken stock
1 cup tomato, chopped
½ pound mushrooms, sliced
2 Tbsp. parsley, chopped
½ tsp. paprika
½ tsp. oregano
½ tsp. basil
1/8 tsp. black pepper

¾ pound boneless chicken breasts,
  trimmed of all fat
½ pound mussels, in their shells
½ pound scallops, shelled
2 cups cooked brown rice

1. Simmer onion and garlic in ¼ cup stock until tender.
2. Add remaining ingredients to onions and garlic. Simmer sauce 20 minutes
3. Cut chicken breasts into bite-size pieces. Add chicken, scallops and mussels to sauce. Simmer 10 minutes.
4. Serve on a bed of rice.

230 Calories per serving

PINEAPPLE-LEMON WHIP

(serves 8)

1 Tbsp. unflavored gelatin
½ cup pineapple juice
1 8-oz. can crushed pineapple in its own
   juice
3 Tbsp. lemon juice
½ cup cold evaporated skim milk
1 Tbsp. sugar
8 strawberries
Mint leaves for garnish

1. Blend gelatin with juice. Heat until gelatin is dissolved.
2. Add pineapple and lemon juice. Refrigerate until thickened, but not stiff.
3. Whip milk until stiff and add sugar gradually as it stiffens. Do not allow this to stand. Use immediately.
4. Fold evaporated milk into pineapple mixture. Pour into sherbet glasses and refrigerate until set.
5. Garnish with a strawberry and mint leaf.

75 Calories per serving

ARRANGED SALAD

½ pound lettuce greens
1 cucumber
1 tomato
Carrot curls

Arrange vegetables attractively on a plate. Use any dressing.

15 Calories per plate

DAY X

Calories		Portions
	BREAKFAST — 220 Calories	
40	Cantaloupe	¼ small
180	French Toast	2 slices
	LUNCH — 295 Calories	
120	East Indian Lentil Soup	6 oz. serving
155	Salade Nicoise	Bowl
20	Flatbread	1
	DINNER — 435 Calories	
55	Vegetable Soup	6 oz. serving
135	Coquilles St. Jacques	2 each
15	Asparagus	4 stalks
160	Two Florence's Fettuccini	1 cup cooked
70	Orange and Grapefruit Ambrosia	½ medium orange ½ small grapefruit
90	Skim Milk	One 8 oz. glass
1040	Calories for the day.	

FRENCH TOAST

(serves 1)

2 slices VERY thin whole wheat bread
1 egg white
¼ cup skim milk
1 tsp. butter or margarine
1 tsp. jelly

1. Whisk egg and milk.
2. Soak bread in mixture until all liquid has been absorbed.
3. Heat pan until a drop of water sizzles. Add one half the butter or margarine and heat again.
4. Place bread slices in pan.
5. Fry to golden brown using only as much of the butter or margarine as you need.

180 Calories for 2 slices

EAST INDIAN LENTIL SOUP

(serves 8)

1 cup dry lentils
1 quart of water to cover

1. The night before you expect to prepare soup, place lentils in 6-quart soup pot. Cover with water and bring to a boil. Allow to boil for 2 minutes. Cover and remove from heat. Let stand overnight.

1 quart of water
2 large soup bones
2 medium onions, minced
3 cloves of garlic, minced
2 tsp. curry powder
½ tsp. chili powder
1/8 tsp. black pepper
2 tsp. lemon juice
2 tsp. lime juice

1 tsp. shredded coconut for each bowl

2. In the morning add the additional water, soup bones, onions, garlic and all seasonings.
3. Cook 1 hour or more until lentils are soft.
4. Serve steaming hot, garnished with shredded coconut.

120 Calories for 6 oz. serving

SALADE NICOISE

(serves 6)

1 head Romaine lettuce
1 head Boston lettuce
1 cucumber, sliced
2 tomatoes, cut into quarters
1 bunch red radishes, cut into slices
1 green pepper, cut into thin strips
4 stalks celery, thinly sliced
1 red onion, thinly sliced
1 cup mushrooms, sliced
2 cups cooked potatoes, thinly sliced

1 7-oz. can water packed tuna
6 artichoke hearts
1 hard cooked egg white
1 cup croutons
  (see BASIC RECIPES)
1 cup vinaigrette dressing
  (see SALAD DRESSINGS)

1. Prepare all vegetables for salad.
2. Drain and flake tuna.
3. Drain and slice artichokes.
4. Toss all ingredients together.
5. Garnish with egg white slices and croutons.

155 Calories per bowl

VEGETABLE SOUP

(serves 8)

4 cups of stock
1 large onion, chopped
2 carrots, diced
1 zucchini, unpeeled, sliced in ¼" slices
2 stalks celery, thinly sliced
¼ pound fresh string beans in ½" pieces
¼ pound fresh peas
1 1-pound can stewed tomatoes, cut up
¼ cup fresh parsley, chopped
1 large potato, peeled and diced
1 tsp. dill weed
¼ tsp. black pepper
¼ tsp. savory
¼ tsp. garlic powder

1. Combine all ingredients, including juice from canned tomatoes.
2. Add seasonings.
3. Bring to boil. Then cook over low heat for one hour.

55 Calories for 6 oz. serving

COQUILLES ST. JACQUES

(serves 6)

1 leek, thinly sliced, including some of the green part
½ small onion, minced
½ cup white wine
½ tsp. marjoram
½ cup evaporated skim milk
½ cup stock
1 Tbsp. cornstarch
1½ pounds bay scallops
1 cup mushrooms, sliced
12 Coquilles (shells)
1 tsp. oil

Topping for Coquilles
3 Tbsp. seasoned breadcrumbs
1 tsp. dried parsley or 1 Tbsp. fresh parsley, minced
Dash black pepper
1 tsp. butter or margarine

1. Simmer onion, leek and marjoram in wine for 5 minutes or until soft.
2. Combine milk, stock and cornstarch in a tightly covered jar. Shake briskly until blended.
3. Cook in small saucepan until thickened. Add to leek, onion and wine mixture.
4. Drain and pat scallops dry. Add scallops and mushrooms to sauce.
5. Simmer for 5 minutes.
6. Rub shells with oil. Distribute mixture into 12 shells.
7. Combine breadcrumbs, seasonings and melted butter. Sprinkle on top of all shells.
8. Bake or broil until hot and bubbly and golden brown. This takes about 10 minutes if you bake, and about 3-4 minutes if you broil.
   Serve immediately with lemon wedge.

135 Calories for 2 coquilles

TWO FLORENCE'S FETTUCCINI

(serves 6)

⅓ pound fettuccini
¼ cup whipped, unsalted butter
¼ cup evaporated skim milk
1 Tbsp. sweet basil
1 Tbsp. fresh parsley, chopped
2 cloves of garlic, finely minced
1/8 tsp. black pepper

1. Cook pasta according to directions.
2. Set a large bowl to warm.
3. Combine butter and skim milk. Whip to double quantity.
4. Add all seasonings to butter.
5. Heat in small saucepan.
6. Drain pasta and place in the warm platter or bowl.
7. Pour butter sauce over pasta and toss.
8. Serve immediately.

160 Calories per serving

ORANGE AND GRAPEFRUIT AMBROSIA

(serves 6)

3 oranges, peeled and segmented
3 grapefruit, peeled and segmented
2 tsp. coconut

1. Place segments of orange and grapefruit on plate.
2. Sprinkle with coconut.

70 Calories per serving

DAY XI

Calories		Portions
	BREAKFAST— 225 Calories	
40	Grapefruit	½ medium
100	Puffed Corn and Granola	1 cup corn plus 2 Tbsp. granola
40	Toast	1 thin size
25	Jelly	1 tsp.
	LUNCH— 270 Calories	
150	Onion Soup	12 oz. serving
80	Tossed Salad with Garbanzo Beans	1/6th recipe
40	Fresh Pineapple	1 thin 3" round
	DINNER— 435 Calories	
80	Clam Chowder	6 oz. serving
145	Seafood en Brochette	4 oz. fish plus vegetables
90	Orzo with Mushrooms	1/6th recipe
25	Broccoli	½ cup cooked
15	Carrot Salad with Bean Sprouts	1/6th recipe
80	Apple Crisp	1/12th recipe

....

Calories		Portions
90	Skim Milk	One 8 oz. glass
1000	Calories for the day.	

GRANOLA

1 1-pound box Rolled Oats
1 cup apple juice, unsweetened

1. Mix oats and apple juice together.
2. Divide into 2 large baking pans and spread over entire bottom of pan.
3. Bake in preheated 250° oven for one hour. Shake pan every 20 minutes or so.
4. Store in a covered container. This is an excellent snack for children since it does not contain all the sugar so many of the commercial types do.

20 Calories per Tbsp.

ONION SOUP

(serves 12)

5 cups onions, thinly sliced
6 cups chicken stock
½ tsp. paprika
¼ tsp. pepper
3 Tbsp. whole wheat flour
½ cup stock
½ cup wine

Croutes
12 slices Italian bread ½″ thick
Garlic powder

To serve
2 oz. Swiss cheese

1. Combine onions, chicken stock and seasonings in a heavy pot and simmer for 30 minutes.
2. Combine flour and stock in a tightly covered jar. Shake vigorously. Add to soup very slowly, stirring constantly.
3. Add wine and simmer slowly 30-40 minutes.
4. Sprinkle bread with a little garlic powder. Bake in a preheated 325° oven for 20-30 minutes or until dried and lightly browned.
5. Ladle soup into individual bowls.
6. Place one croute on each bowl of soup and top with a small piece of cheese.
7. Bake for 10 minutes or until cheese melts. Place under broiler for one or two minutes. Serve immediately.

75 Calories for 6 oz. serving
When the soup is used as the main dish of a light meal, double the quantity served and use it for six people.

TOSSED SALAD WITH GARBANZO BEANS

(serves 6)

1 head Boston lettuce
1 head Romaine lettuce
1 cucumber, thinly sliced
1 red onion, thinly sliced
1 green pepper, cut into small strips
1 tomato cut into quarters
1 cup cooked garbanzo beans, drained
1 cup lemon-vinegar dressing
  (see SALAD DRESSINGS)

1. Shred lettuce. Toss all ingredients with dressing.

80 Calories per serving

CLAM CHOWDER

(serves 6)

2 tomatoes cut in cubes
1 1-pound can tomatoes, chopped
2 cups stock
1 cup onion, chopped
½ cup celery, chopped
2 Tbsp. tomato paste
1 cup potatoes, cubed
2 Tbsp. parsley
2 cloves garlic, finely chopped
¼ tsp. rough cut black pepper
¼ tsp. thyme
1 Tbsp. celery seed
2 dozen small clams or 12 large ones

1. Place all ingredients except clams in a heavy pot. Simmer covered for 45 minutes to one hour.
2. Steam clams until they open up. Remove meat and cut into small pieces. Add to soup and simmer 5 minutes more.

80 Calories per serving

SEAFOOD EN BROCHETTE

(serves 6)

1½ pounds halibut

Marinade
¼ cup white wine
2 Tbsp. lemon juice
1 tsp. fresh dill or dill weed
1/8 tsp. pepper

2 tomatoes cut into cubes
12 small onions, left whole
2 green peppers cut into strips

1. Cut halibut into cubes.
2. Combine all marinade ingredients. Marinate cubes for 30 minutes. Reserve some marinade for vegetables.
3. Parboil onions ten minutes. Place in marinade.
4. Place fish and vegetables on skewers alternating fish and vegetables. Brush marinade on vegetables.
5. Barbecue over hot coals five minutes on each side, or broil in oven for 5 minutes on each side.

145 Calories per serving

ORZO

(serves 6)

3 oz. Orzo
2 Tbsp. onion, finely chopped
1 cup mushrooms, sliced
1 Tbsp. oil

1. Cook orzo according to directions on package.

2. Heat pan until a drop of water sizzles. Add oil. When oil sizzles saute onions until golden brown. Add mushrooms and saute 2 minutes. Add onions and mushrooms to Orzo.

90 Calories per serving

CARROT SALAD WITH BEAN SPROUTS

(serves 6)

2 carrots, peeled
½ cup bean sprouts washed in cold water. Pat dry.

1. Shred carrots, do not chop
2. Combine carrots and bean sprouts.
3. Toss with vinaigrette dressing. (see SALAD DRESSINGS)

15 Calories per serving

APPLE CRISP

(serves 12)

6 medium table apples
2 Tbsp. lemon juice
½ cup cold water
½ cup whole wheat flour
1 Tbsp. sugar
1 tsp. cinnamon
1 Tbsp. butter or margarine

1. Peel and core apples. Cut into 8ths and then cut in half. Immediately sprinkle with 2 Tbsp. lemon juice and toss.
2. Combine flour, sugar, cinnamon and butter. Mix with fork as you would a pie crust to blend butter with flour.
3. Spread apples onto bottom of flat, oblong baking dish.
4. Pour the water alond sides to reach botto of pan under apples.
5. Sprinkle dry ingredients over top of apples. Use a fork to move apple around in the pan to be sure the dry mixture reaches all the apples.
6. Sprinkle with a little more cinnamon if you like.
7. Bake in preheated 350° oven for 1 hour, or until golden brown and bubbling.
8. Remove from oven and let "set" for about 10 minutes. Serve hot.

80 Calories per serving

DAY XII

Calories		Portions
	BREAKFAST — 210 Calories	
80	Orange Rounds	1 orange
110	Cornmeal Pancakes	1/6th recipe
20	Strawberry Sauce	3 Tbsp.
	LUNCH — 285 Calories	
75	Fresh Minted Pea Soup	6 oz. serving
80	Spanakopita (Spinach Pie)	1/6th recipe
45	Grilled Tomato	½ medium
85	Stewed Pears	1 medium
	DINNER — 485 Calories	
40	Ikra (Eggplant Caviar)	1/6th recipe
275	Russian Borsch	10 oz. serving
80	Black Bread	1 slice
70	Apple Blini	1
20	Fruit Sauce	1½ Tbsp.
90	Skim Milk	One 8 oz. glass
1070	Calories for the day.	

ORANGE ROUNDS

(serves 1)

1 medium orange

1. Peel and slice crosswise.
2. Garnish with a mint leaf.

80 Calories per serving

ROUMANIAN CORNMEAL CAKES WITH STRAWBERRIES

(serves 6)

1 cup cornmeal
1 tsp. oil

Topping
1 pt. strawberries, cleaned
1 cup water

1. Prepare cornmeal according to directions on box. Do NOT add salt.
2. Refrigerate in loaf pan for several hours or overnight, until firm.
3. Remove carefully to keep shape. Slice into thin slices.
4. Moisten cookie sheet with oil. Place cornmeal slices on sheet and bake in preheated 350° oven for 15 minutes.
5. Simmer strawberries until soft. Serve hot over cornmeal cakes.

110 Calories per serving cornmeal
20 Calories for 3 Tbsp. strawberries

FRESH MINTED PEA SOUP

(serves 6)

1 pound peas, shelled or frozen
1 onion, chopped
1 stalk celery, cut in pieces
4 cups chicken or vegetable stock
2 Tbsp. fresh chopped mint leaves, or 1½ tsp. dried
1/8 tsp. black pepper

1. Simmer all ingredients in a heavy covered saucepan until vegetables are tender.
2. Cool and puree in a blender.
3. Return to saucepan. Adjust seasonings and simmer until hot.
4. Serve with a dollop of yogurt.

75 Calories for 6 oz. serving

SPANOKOPITA

(serves 6)

1 10-oz. package frozen leaf spinach
3 egg whites
1 cup skim milk
2 oz. Swiss cheese
1/8 tsp. black pepper
1/8 tsp. nutmeg
¼ cup skim milk
2 Tbsp. whole wheat flour
1 tsp. oil
1/8 tsp. nutmeg

1. Steam spinach. Drain well by pressing down in strainer to eliminate all liquid. Cool slightly.
2. Beat egg whites lightly. Add milk to egg whites and mix. Add cheese, pepper and nutmeg.
3. Mix milk and flour together in a tightly covered jar. Shake vigorously. Do not heat. Add to milk, egg and cheese mixture. Mix well together.
4. Grease the pan. Pour about half the sauce into the pan.
5. Distribute the strained and cooled spinach over the sauce.
6. Pour the remaining sauce over spinach.
7. Sprinkle the nutmeg on top. Bake in preheated 350° oven for 45 minutes or until set and golden brown.
8. Allow to set after removing from oven for about 10 minutes. Serve while hot.

80 Calories for 1/6th of pie

GRILLED TOMATOES

(serves 6)

3 medium tomatoes
¼ cup seasoned bread crumbs
1 Tbsp. melted butter or margarine
1 Tbsp. parsley, minced

1. Cut tomatoes in half, crosswise.
2. Combine bread crumbs and melted butter. Spread evenly over tomatoes and sprinkle with parsley.
3. Bake in preheated 350° oven for 25-30 minutes.

45 Calories per serving

STEWED PEARS

(serves 6)

6 ripe medium pears
½ cup unsweetened pineapple juice
3 Tbsp. lemon juice
1 tsp. cinnamon

1. Cut pears in half and core them. Cut in eighths and place them in saucepan.
2. Mix juices together and pour over pears. Sprinkle with cinnamon. Simmer slowly about 20 minutes or until soft. Serve warm.

85 Calories per serving

IKRA (EGGPLANT CAVIAR)

(serves 8)

1 medium eggplant
1 medium zucchini
1 tomato
1 large green pepper, finely chopped
2 small onions, finely chopped
1 cup tomato sauce
3 cloves garlic, minced
¼ tsp. black pepper
¼ tsp. sweet basil
1 Tbsp. wine vinegar

1. Peel and cut eggplant into small pieces.
2. Wash and cut zucchini into small pieces.
3. Cut tomato into small pieces
4. Combine all ingredients. Simmer for one hour, and then cool.
5. Refrigerate overnight. Serve in lettuce cups.

40 Calories per serving
NOTE: This recipe makes a very nice *hors d'oeuvre*

BORSCH

(serves 12)

½ cup lima beans
½ cup kidney beans
½ cup pearled barley
3 quarts water
1½ pounds lean meat
2 onions, chopped
3 cloves garlic, minced
2 carrots, diced
2 stalks celery, sliced
1½ pounds cabbage, shredded
2 cups juilienne beets with juice
1 1-pound can tomatoes, chopped
½ cup red wine
2 bay leaves (to be removed later)
½ cup parsley, chopped
6 black peppercorns
1 tsp. black pepper
2 tsp. garlic powder
6 Tbsp. lemon juice
3 small potatoes, diced

1. Place beans and barley in a large pot and cover with water. Bring to a boil. Turn off flame and soak overnight.
2. The next day, add meat, vegetables, wine and seasonings to beans. Cook 2-2½ hours. Skim foam and stir from time to time.
3. Add potatoes for last 45 minutes of cooking period. Soup must be cooked until beans are soft.
4. When soup is finished, remove bay leaves. Chill thoroughly in order to skim off congealed fat. There should be very little if the meat is lean.

We suggest you prepare this soup at least a day before you plan to serve it.

275 Calories for 10 oz. serving

APPLE BLINI

(serves 16)

4 egg whites
1½ cups skim milk
1 cup whole wheat flour
2 tsp. baking powder
1½ tsp. oil

1. Combine milk and eggs.
2. Sift flour and baking powder together.
3. Add to egg-milk mixture and beat until smooth.
4. Pre-heat crepe pan. (A good coated pan is essential.) When a drop of water sizzles, brush pan with a little oil.
5. Pour in about 2 Tbsp. batter and tilt so entire bottom is covered. Fry for about one minute.
6. Turn out onto clean kitchen towel, done side down.

Filling

3 cups apples, chopped
3 Tbsp. orange juice
1 tsp. cinnamon
1 tsp. lemon juice
½ cup raisins
½ tsp. oil
2 Tbsp. skim milk

1. Simmer apples in orange juice until tender.
2. Add cinnamon, lemon juice and raisins to apples.
3. Divide filling evenly onto blini. Fold in thirds. Do not tuck in ends.
4. Grease baking pan. Brush blini with skim milk. Bake in preheated 400° oven for 10 minutes.

70 Calories per blini

Orange Sauce for Apple Blini

1 cup unsweetened orange juice
1 Tbsp. lemon juice
1 Tbsp. honey
¼ cup cold water
1½ Tbsp. flour
3 Tbsp. Cointreau

1. Heat orange juice, lemon juice and honey together for five minutes on low flame.
2. Prepare a paste with flour and water. Stir paste into sauce and cook over low heat until thickened.
3. Add Cointreau and stir.
4. Place blini in a baking pan. Pour sauce over blini. Bake in preheated 350° oven for 10-15 minutes.

20 Calories per 1½ Tbsp. sauce

DAY XIII

Calories		Portions
	BREAKFAST — 265 Calories	
80	Orange Slices	1 medium
125	California Omelet	1 egg plus vegetables
40	Whole Wheat Bread	1 very thin slice
20	Jelly	1 tsp
	LUNCH — 255 Calories	
200	Timballo Alla Firenze (Vegetable Lasagne)	1/6th recipe
15	Hearts of Lettuce with Carrot Curls	1/6th head
40	Honeydew with Lime Wedge	2″ wedge
	DINNER — 425 Calories	
75	Cream of Tomato-Celery Soup	6 oz. serving
150	Batter Fried Fish	2 small fillets
50	Potato Chips	1 very small potato
50	Harvard Beets	½ cup
30	Cabbage and Apple Salad	1/6th recipe
70	Peach Fluff	1/6th recipe

....

90	Skim Milk	One 8 oz. glass
1035	Calories for the day.	

CALIFORNIA OMELET

(serves 1)

2 Tbsp. onion, thinly sliced
¼ green pepper, thinly sliced
2 Tbsp. water
Dash black pepper
1 whole egg
1 tsp. butter or margarine

1. Simmer onions and green pepper in water until onions become transparent.
2. Heat small frying pan and add 1 tsp. butter or margarine.
3. Whisk egg. Pour into heated pan. Allow to just set. Add onions and green pepper mixture to one-half of omelet. Fold other half over the filling. Cover pan and turn heat off. Allow to stand three minutes until set.

125 Calories per serving

TIMBALLO ALLA FIRENZE

(serves 6)

8 oz. lasagne noodles
1 Tbsp. oil
1 cup zucchini, chopped
1 cup fresh broccoli, chopped
1 clove garlic, minced
1 medium onion, chopped
1 1-pound can plum tomatoes, chopped
¼ tsp. each of oregano, basil, garlic powder, black pepper and crushed red pepper

2 Tbsp. Parmesan cheese

1. Prepare noodles according to directions on the package. Do not add salt to the water.
2. Heat pan until a drop of water sizzles. Add oil; heat again. Saute garlic and onions until golden brown. Add zucchini and broccoli and stir fry 3 minutes.
3. Add tomatoes and seasonings. Cook at low boil for ten minutes in a covered pan. *Do not overcook.* Vegetables should be crunchy.

Assemblage:

1. Spoon a small amount of sauce in bottom of 2-quart round casserole. Cut noodles to fit pan. Starting with noodles in first layer, alternate noodles and sauce. Finish with sauce on the top.
2. Sprinkle cheese on top of sauce. Bake in preheated 350° oven for 20-30 minutes.
3. Allow to set for five minutes. Cut in pie wedges to serve.

200 Calories per serving

CREAM OF TOMATO-CELERY SOUP

(serves 6)

1 1-pound can crushed tomatoes
2 cups celery, sliced in small pieces
1 onion, chopped
½ tsp. thyme
1 tsp. basil
3 cloves
1 tsp. sugar

2 Tbsp flour
½ cup skim milk
1 cup evaporated skim milk

1. Combine all ingredients except flour and milk in a heavy pot and simmer covered for 45 minutes to one hour.
2. Combine flour and milk by shaking vigorously in a tightly covered jar. Add to hot soup very slowly, stirring constantly.
3. Simmer five more minutes.

75 Calories per serving

HEARTS OF LETTUCE WITH CARROT CURLS

(serves 6)

1 large head lettuce
1 carrot, peeled

1. Cut lettuce into six wedges.

2. Shave thin strips of carrot with vegetable peeler. Drop into ice water until strips curl. Arrange over hearts of lettuce.

15 Calories per serving

BATTER FRIED FISH 'N CHIPS

(serves 6)

2 Tbsp. whole wheat pancake flour
2 Tbsp. milk
1½ pounds flounder fillets (12 pieces)
1 Tbsp. oil

1. Make a batter of milk and flour. Use a little more milk if necessary.

2. Spread batter over fish fillets.
3. Heat pan until a drop of water sizzles. Add oil and heat again. Saute fillets on both sides until brown. This takes about three minutes for each side.

150 Calories for 2 fillets

POTATO CHIPS

(serves 6)

(This can be done very nicely in a toaster oven for one or two small potatoes. This is a great recipe for kids, too, and much better than potato chips with all their oil and salt.)

1 pound potatoes, thin skinned
½ tsp. oil

1. Scrub potatoes. Slice into 1/8" slices.
2. Lightly oil baking pan and place sliced potatoes in a single layer in the pan.
3. Bake in preheated 450° oven 20 minutes or until brown. Serve *immediately.*

50 Calories for 1/6th recipe

CABBAGE-APPLE SALAD WITH YOGURT DRESSING

(serves 6)

1 medium apple
½ pound red cabbage

Dressing
4 Tbsp. low fat plain yogurt
1 tsp. prepared mustard
1/8 tsp. black pepper

1. Cut apple into small pieces. Do not peel.
2. Shred cabbage, do not chop.
3. Toss together.
4. Combine yogurt, mustard and black pepper for dressing. Pour over apple-cabbage mixture. Toss. Allow to stand for at least two hours before serving.

30 Calories per serving

HARVARD BEETS

(serves 6)

½ cup pineapple juice
2 Tbsp. cornstarch
½ cup juice from beets
3 cups sliced beets

1. Combine pineapple juice and cornstarch. Blend well and add to beet juice.
2. Heat until the sauce thickens, stirring constantly. Add beets to sauce and heat for a few minutes more.
3. Serve warm or chilled as vegetable or relish.

50 Calories per serving

PEACH FLUFF

(serves 6)

2 cups cooked peaches
½ cup orange juice
2 Tbsp. lemon juice
1 Tbsp. gelatin

1. Puree peaches in blender.
2. Sprinkle gelatin over juice. Heat until gelatin is dissolved, stirring constantly.
3. Combine with peaches.
4. Pour into six sherbet glasses. Top with a fresh mint leaf.
5. Refrigerate until set.

70 Calories for 1/6th recipe
Use waterpacked peaches or ones packed in their own juice. If you use fresh peaches, use six medium ones.

DAY XIV

Calories		Portions
	BREAKFAST—230 Calories	
150	Fruit 'N Cottage Cheese Plate	½ orange
		½ small banana
		¼ cup cottage cheese
80	Miniature Bagel	1
	LUNCH—230 Calories	
125	Mexicali Bean Soup	1/12 recipe
20	Spinach and Mushroom Salad	A few leaves with 1/8th cup mushrooms
35	Bread Stick, Whole Wheat	1
50	Grapefruit and Kiwi Sections	½ small grapefruit
		¼ kiwi
	DINNER—455 Calories	
25	Tossed Salad	1 bowl
285	Roast Veal	3 oz. serving
60	Rack Roasted Potato	1
25	Julienne Carrots with Mint	½ cup
60	Stewed Fresh Apricots	1/6th recipe
90	Skim Milk	One 8 oz. glass
1005	Calories for the day.	

FRUIT 'N COTTAGE CHEESE PLATE

(serves 6)

3 oranges
3 small bananas
1½ cups low fat cottage cheese

Arrange orange segments and banana slices attractively around a small mound of cottage cheese.

150 Calories per serving

MEXICALI BEAN SOUP

(serves 12)

½ cup dried red kidney beans
½ cup dried chick peas
2 quarts chicken or vegetable stock
1 1-pound can plum tomatoes
2 onions
½ bunch celery with leaves
3 carrots
¼ cup Italian parsley
½ cup string beans
½ tsp. black pepper
2 oz. small macaroni

1. Place both red beans and chick peas in a large pot. Cover with water (about 1 quart) and bring to a boil. Cool, and soak overnight.
2. Chop all vegetables uniformly and add to stock.
3. Add beans, including bean water.
4. Add seasonings and cook, tightly covered, for one hour.
5. Add uncooked macaroni to soup. Cook 15 minutes more. Stir well and serve very hot.

125 Calories per serving

SPINACH-MUSHROOM SALAD

(serves 6)

½ pound spinach
½ pound mushrooms, sliced
¼ red onion, thinly sliced in rings

1. Wash and dry fresh spinach.
2. Arrange mushrooms attractively over spinach.
3. Add sliced onion rings.
4. Toss with vinaigrette dressing (see SALAD DRESSINGS).

20 Calories for 1/6th recipe

VEAL ROAST

2½ pounds veal shoulder

Marinade
½ cup rose wine
½ cup stock
2 onions, sliced in rings
2 cloves garlic, crushed
1 bay leaf
½ tsp. black pepper

(serves 8)

1. Combine all ingredients for marinade.
2. Marinate veal 24 hours, turning frequently.
3. Place in a baking pan on a rack. Cover top with foil tent. Bake in a preheated 325° oven for one hour. Uncover and bake for another 30-45 minutes or until tender. Baste with marinade.

285 Calories per serving

RACK ROASTED POTATO

6 small potatoes

(serves 6)

1. Peel potatoes.
2. Place on rack with veal.

60 calories per serving

JULIENNE CARROTS WITH MINT

5 carrots, peeled
2 tsp. fresh mint, or 1 tsp. dried

(serves 6)

1. Clean and cut carrots into thin strips.
2. Steam carrots with mint. Do not overcook.

25 Calories per serving

STEWED FRESH APRICOTS
WITH CHERRY WINE

(serves 6)

12 fresh apricots, pitted
2 Tbsp. lemon juice
Dash cinnamon
½ cup cherry wine

1. Combine all ingredients.
2. Simmer, covered, for 30 minutes.
3. Add a little water, if necessary.

60 Calories per serving

planning your meals

We have given you the tools-of-the-trade. You know the how and why. Now you must learn the shoulds and the oughts. The methodology in our cuisine is what you have absorbed in the past Fourteen Days. The way you prepare food, the amount in each portions and the ingredients you use are basic training for your future. Good nutrition will now be second nature to you. Excessive amounts of fat for frying should repel you, fast foods will turn you off, but you will have acquired a palate for full course meals, international dishes, easy to prepare soups and interesting salads.

Your new knowledge will be applied to the following section. You are now on your own, making selections from the food groups and using the Fourteen Day Plan as a guide. Remember, you can now increase your caloric intake by at least 200 calories. Use them wisely and well. We have previously not allowed for wine and liquors in our menus as a beverage, but you may now enjoy a glass of wine. A dry white wine has about 90 calories for 3½ ounces. Budget it in, if you wish, or opt for one of the new "light wines" on the market. They claim to have one-third less calories. Keep in mind that these are really empty calories. Enjoy it, though there is no known nourishment. A better choice for instance would be a fruit for about 60 calories, or a slice of very thin sliced whole wheat bread for 40 calories, etc., but the choice is now yours.

Plan your breakfast well. Make it as complete a meal as any other. Two hundred to two hundred and fifty calories will keep you virtually hunger-free until lunch. Then try for the same number of calories for lunch. A soup and salad luncheon is a marvelous combination, — satisfying and nutritionally sound.

Your late afternoon slumps can be picked up with the extra allowable calories. Munch on some of the salad greens as you prepare dinner, or sneak some of your dinner soup while you do your preparation to cut down on your hunger. Prepare your dinner with tender loving care. Make it attractive. Enjoy that beautiful bowl of salad before the entree, another way to assuage your hunger. Concentrate on your portion control . . . that's how calories are controlled. Be sure to start out with a food scale. By this time you should be able to judge your portions, but once in a while, go back, weigh and measure. You are only fooling yourself if you don't check. Have a hot beverage following dinner and reserve whatever you have planned for dessert for your before-bed-snack, if you think you will need that. Or close the kitchen after dinner and forget it's there.

It may have been fun getting through the Fourteen Days, but it could not have been easy. Don't spoil it now. Plan ahead in your shopping, having everything you need in the house so you will not have to substitute . . . and keep in control!

basic recipes

The few recipes in this section will become regulars and committed to your memory in short order. We know it is easier to buy commercial yogurt, but it is almost impossible to find low-fat skim milk yogurt; we know seasoned bread crumbs are available, but they contain salt, and the same goes for croutons. So, make the effort; all of the suggested Basic Recipes can be made in advance and stored for long periods of time. Avail yourself of these and save the short-cuts for the road.

SEASONED BREAD CRUMBS

To be used sparingly; each tablespoon has 22 calories.

1 cup plain bread crumbs
1 tsp. oregano
1 tsp. dried sweet basil
1 tsp. dried parsley flakes
½ tsp. garlic powder
¼ tsp. black pepper

345 Calories per cup

SPICE BLEND

Can be combined and placed in shaker on the table for those who are accustomed to reaching for salt.

1 tsp. garlic powder
1 tsp. powdered mustard
2 tsp. onion powder
1 tsp. curry powder
1 tsp. white pepper
½ tsp. cumin
1 tsp. black pepper

HOME-MADE YOGURT

4 cups low-fat skim milk
2 Tbsp. instant fat-free dry milk
2 Tbsp. commercial plain low-fat yogurt
  with live culture

NOTE: After your first batch you can use
  your own yogurt as "starter," but you must
  start with a commercial yogurt with live
  culture.

1. Combine milk and instant dry milk.
2. Bring just to the boiling point on
    medium flame.
3. Remove from heat, stir, and allow to
    cool until luke-warm.
4. Add commercial yogurt and stir.
5. Store in warm place until mixture
    reaches consistency of cream.
6. Pour into container and refrigerate.

Yield: 4 cups
100 Calories per cup

CROUTONS

2 slices of very thin-sliced whole wheat
  bread
1 tsp. butter or margarine
Dash of black pepper
Dash of garlic powder

1. Toast bread until golden brown.
2. Spread butter or margarine over both
    slices.

3. Sprinkle with black pepper and garlic
    powder.
4. Cut slices into 1-inch cubes.
5. Toss and spread out on baking pan.
6. Return to oven for a few minutes until
    crisp.

40 Calories each slice of bread
35 Calories for 1 tsp. butter

BUTTER BLEND I

¼ pound sweet butter
½ cup evaporated skim milk

Whip butter and milk together in a blender.

75 Calories per Tbsp.

BUTTER BLEND II

¼ pound sweet butter
½ cup oil

Whip butter and oil together in a blender.

100 Calories per Tbsp.

These butter blends are offered to those
who do not wish to use pure butter because
of its cholesterol or saturated fat content,
and wish to avoid magarine because of its additives.

salad dressings

Salad dressings should be prepared several hours before using to allow the flavors to blend. Store in a tightly covered jar. Shake well before using. Large quantities of your favorite dressings can be prepared by doubling or tripling the recipe. Keep in the refrigerator for future use.

COTTAGE CHEESE DRESSING

½ cup low-fat cottage cheese
1 cup low-fat plain yogurt
1 tsp. sugar
4 tsp. lemon juice
½ cup skim milk

Place all ingredients in a blender and whip at high speed.

Yield: about 2 cups
8 Calories per Tbsp.
A fine dressing for fruit salads.

CREAMY ONION DRESSING

1 medium onion, chopped
2 stalks celery, chopped
1 tsp. parsley, chopped
2 Tbsp. low-fat plain yogurt
½ cup water
½ cup wine vinegar
¼ tsp. black pepper
½ tsp. each basil, garlic powder, oregano

Puree all ingredients in a blender.

Yield: about 1½ cups
3 Calories per Tbsp.

"FAKE" MAYONNAISE

½ cup skim evaporated milk
½ cup oil
1 egg white
1 tsp. dry mustard
1 tsp. white vinegar
1 Tbsp. lemon juice
Dash cayenne pepper

Blend all ingredients in a blender at high speed until the mayonnaise thickens.

Yield: 1 cup
70 Calories per Tbsp.
We offer this recipe not for the person who is on a low-calorie diet, but for someone who is on a salt-free diet. This mayonnaise also has no additives or preservatives.

FRENCH DRESSING

1 cup tomato juice
¾ cup orange juice
¼ cup apple cider vinegar
½ tsp. dry mustard
½ tsp. onion powder
¼ tsp. tumeric
¼ tsp. unflavored gelatin
¼ tsp. celery seed
2 Tbsp. fresh parsley, chopped

Combine all ingredients in a sauce-pan. Bring to a boil and simmer for 2-3 minutes. Cool. Refrigerate.

Yield: 2 cups
5 Calories per Tbsp.

LEMON-VINEGAR DRESSING

½ cup water
¼ cup tarragon vinegar
¼ cup lemon juice
1 tsp. sugar
½ tsp. each basil, chives, parsley, oregano
½ tsp. garlic powder
½ tsp. Dijon mustard
¼ tsp. fresh ground black pepper

Combine all ingredients in a jar. Shake well.

Yield: 1 cup
No calories worth talking about

NOTE: When fresh herbs are available, use 1 Tbsp. of each. Mince them and place all ingredients in a blender for one minute.

ITALIAN DRESSING

½ cup red wine vinegar
½ cup cold water
1 tsp. sugar
¼ tsp. each black pepper, sweet basil,
    garlic powder, oregano, dried parsley

Combine all ingredients in a jar. Shake vigorously.

Yield: 1 cup
No Calories worth talking about

POPPY SEED DRESSING

½ cup low-fat cottage cheese
¼ cup water
2 Tbsp. white wine vinegar
3 Tbsp. lemon juice
1 tsp. prepared mustard
1 Tbsp. poppy seeds

Place all ingredients except poppy seeds in a blender and whip at high speed. Add poppy seeds afterwards.

Yield: 1 cup
5 Calories per Tbsp.

TANGY BOILED DRESSING

1 Tbsp. cornstarch
½ tsp. Dijon mustard
1 cup cold water
¼ cup wine vinegar
½ tsp. each
  prepared horseradish
  paprika
  sugar
  Worcesteshire sauce
1 clove garlic, minced

Mix cornstarch and mustard. Gradually stir in water. Place in a small saucepan and cook over medium heat until thickened, stirring constantly.
Add vinegar and spices. Mix well. Cool.

Yield: 1½ cups
No calories worth talking about

TARRAGON TOMATO DRESSING

1 cup tomato sauce
2 Tbsp. tarragon vinegar
1 tsp. Worcesteshire sauce
½ tsp. each onion powder, dill seed,
  sweet basil
1/8 tsp. black pepper

Combine all ingredients in a jar. Shake vigorously. Allow to stand at room temperature for four hours or longer. Chill.

Yield: about 1 cup.
5 Calories per Tbsp.

THOUSAND ISLAND DRESSING

1 cup low-fat plain yogurt
2 Tbsp. chili sauce
½ green pepper, chopped fine
½ small onion, chopped fine
1 tsp. dill weed

1 Tbsp. dried vegetable flakes, crushed
1/8 tsp. black pepper

Combine all ingredients and mix well.

Yield: about 1 cup.
10 Calories per Tbsp.

VINAIGRETTE DRESSING

½ cup water
¼ cup white wine vinegar
¼ cup lime juice
½ tsp. garlic powder
½ tsp. dry mustard
¼ tsp. black pepper
1 Tbsp. oil

Combine all ingredients in a jar. Shake vigorously.

Yield: 1 cup
8 Calories per Tbsp.

VARIATIONS: Add 1 tsp. fresh chopped parsley and basil.
Add ¼ tsp. tarragon.

YOGURT DRESSING I

1 cup low-fat plain yogurt
2 Tbsp. dry vermouth
1 tsp. dry mustard
1 tsp. lemon juice
1 tsp. onion juice
¼ tsp. garlic powder
¼ tsp. dried dill

1 Tbsp. fresh parsley, chopped
1/8 tsp. black pepper

Combine all ingredients in a jar. Shake vigorously.

Yield: about 1 cup
9 Calories per Tbsp.

YOGURT DRESSING II

¾ cup low-fat plain yogurt
¼ cup skim milk
1 tsp. onion juice
½ tsp. dry mustard
½ tsp. garlic powder
¼ tsp. dried dill or 1 tsp. fresh dill

1 tsp. parsley, chopped
1/8 tsp. black pepper

Combine all ingredients in a jar. Shake vigorously.

Yield: 1 cup
6 Calories per Tbsp.

YOGURT CUCUMBER DRESSING

1 cup low-fat plain yogurt
1 cucumber
¼ tsp. dried mint
1 Tbsp. dry vermouth
1/8 tsp. black pepper

Peel cucumber. Cut in half length-wise. Remove seeds and pat dry. Cut in slices. Combine all ingredients in a blender. Whip until smooth.

Yield: 1½ cups
7 Calories per Tbsp.

sauces

This section offers you a few surprises. Hollandaise Sauce is our special gift to you; it tastes, looks and is real. We do not use any "instant" anything, no substitutes and nothing artificial, and ours is *good*. So are the Bechamel Sauce and the Newberg Sauce. These and others are usually unheard of in diet cookbooks. We feel they are important so long as the portion control is followed. Many foods are enhanced by sauces, but there is no need to use heavy cream and loads of butter to achieve a good result.

basic sauces

BASIC WHITE SAUCE

	Flour	Skim milk	Calories
Thin	1 Tbsp.	1 cup	115
Medium	2 Tbsp.	1 cup	140
Thick	3 Tbsp.	1 cup	165

1. Combine flour and milk in tightly covered jar.
2. Shake vigorously until blended for no-lump sauce.
3. Heat slowly, stirring constantly until thickened.
4. Add a dash of black pepper.

VARIATIONS:
1. Add ¼ tsp. curry powder for different taste.
2. Add ¼ tsp. dill weed for variety.

BARBECUE SAUCE

1 8-oz. can crushed pineapple with juice (canned in its own juice)
1 cup tomato sauce
1 tsp. chili powder
½ tsp. garlic powder
½ tsp. dry mustard
½ tsp. black pepper
¼ tsp. ginger, powdered or ground
2 Tbsp. lemon juice

1. Cook all ingredients for 15 minutes.
2. Stir from time to time.
3. Can be cooled and stored.

Serve over steaks or use to marinate chicken, fish or vegetables.

Yield: 2 cups
55 Calories per ½ cup

BECHAMEL SAUCE

2 cups basic medium white sauce
¼ cup Parmesan cheese
2 egg whites, whisked
1/8 tsp. black pepper

1. Add cheese to heated basic white sauce.
2. Add egg whites slowly, mixing briskly as you add them.
3. Sprinkle with black pepper.

Serve on eggplant, veal, chicken, etc.

Yield: 2 cups
104 Calories per ½ cup

FAKE SOUR CREAM

1 cup low-fat cottage cheese
2 Tbsp. white wine vinegar
3 Tbsp. skim evaporated milk

1. Use electric beater to blend all ingredients together until smooth.
2. Chill before serving.

VARIATIONS:
1. Add 2 tsp. chopped chives.
2. Add 1 Tbsp. chopped fresh parsley.

Serve on baked potatoes, chopped mixed fresh vegetables, cold soups or use as a dip.

Yield: 1 full cup
14 Calories per Tbsp.

HOLLANDAISE SAUCE

1 Tbsp. mayonnaise
1 Tbsp. melted margarine
3 Tbsp. lemon juice
3 Tbsp. cold water

1. Heat all ingredients together until well blended.
2. Serve immediately over asparagus, broccoli, etc.

Yield: ½ cup
17 Calories per tsp.

MUSHROOM SAUCE

2 cups of basic medium white sauce
½ cup onions, chopped
¼ cup water for simmering
10 oz. mushrooms, sliced
1/8 tsp. black pepper

1. Combine onions and water and simmer 10 minutes.
2. Add to heated white sauce.
3. Add sliced mushrooms and cook 5 minutes.
4. Continue to stir and heat until desired thickness has been reached.

Serve over rice, pasta, noodles, leftover chicken, turkey, vegetables, etc.

Yield: 2 cups
95 Calories per ½ cup

MUSTARD SAUCE

1 cup low-fat plain yogurt
3 Tbsp. dill, chopped
½ tsp. sugar
2 Tbsp. Dijon mustard
1/8 tsp. black pepper
2 Tbsp. red wine vinegar

1. Place all ingredients in tightly covered jar.
2. Shake vigorously until well blended.
3. Store in refrigerator.

Yield: 1 cup
5 Calories per Tbsp.

NEWBERG SAUCE

2 Tbsp. mayonnaise
½ cup evaporated skim milk
¼ cup dry sherry wine
1/8 tsp. white pepper
Dash nutmeg
¼ cup Parmesan cheese

1. Combine all ingredients and heat together until well blended.
2. Stir and simmer for 5 minutes.

Serve by Tbsp. over fish, vegetables, chicken, seafood or serve cold over salad vegetables.

Yield: 1 scant cup
30 Calories per Tbsp.

TOMATO SAUCE

2 small onions, chopped
¼ cup water for simmering
1 28-oz. can of mashed tomatoes or the
    equivalent in cooked fresh tomatoes,
    both with juice
½ tsp. dried sweet basil
½ tsp. oregano
1/8 tsp. black pepper
½ tsp. garlic powder
1 tsp. sugar
2 Tbsp. red wine vinegar
2 sprigs fresh parsley, chopped

1. Simmer onions in water.
2. Add mashed tomatoes and water or juice from tomatoes, and all seasonings.
3. Bring to a low boil. Reduce heat and cook for 30 minutes.
4. Stir from time to time.

Yield: 3 cups
105 Calories per cup

WHITE WINE SAUCE

1 Tbsp. cornstarch
½ cup dry white wine
½ cup cold water
½ tsp. Worcestershire Sauce
1 green onion with stem, chopped

1. Mix cornstarch with wine and water. Blend while cold.
2. Heat in saucepan, then add the Worcestershire Sauce and the green onion.
3. Cook for 5 to 7 minutes.

Serve over chicken, fish, vegetables, etc.

Yield: 1 cup
8 Calories per Tbsp.

stocks

Our cuisine and our cooking methods call for a lot of Stocks. We use them to simmer vegetables, for preparing soups and sauces, for poaching fish and for liquid in many cases where other recipes call for fat. Using stock instead of water enhances flavor, instead of thinning it. The most useful of all is, of course, the chicken stock. Remember that the chicken, cooled and boned is great for freezing to be used later in salads as well as for quick and easy casseroles.

Be sure to cool and then chill your stocks to remove ALL visible fat from the surface. If you prepare a large amount of stock, freeze it in small containers for quick soups. If you have a good rich stock, all you need to add are some vegetables and beans and you have a dinner soup.

basic stocks

CHICKEN STOCK

4 carrots, sliced
4 stalks celery with leaves, sliced
3 onions, sliced
2 leeks, sliced (optional)
1 parsnip (optional)
1 5-pound fowl or equivalent in carcass,
   backs, wings and necks
4 quarts water
¼ tsp. black pepper

1. Place chicken in 4 quarts of cold water and bring to a boil. Skim water after 10 minutes of cooking.
2. Add onions, black pepper and parsnip and simmer for 2 hours. Skim again.

3. Add vegetables and cook for 1 hour. Remove from heat. Cool and refrigerate for several hours, then skim fat and discard it.

Reserve chicken meat for salad or casserole. The stock can be frozen or refrigerated for future use.

Yield: 3 quarts
25 Calories per cup

NOTE: This is the basic stock referred to in our recipes. No-salt, very low-fat chicken stock is available in health food stores. Approximately 12 calories per cup. CAUTION: Do not buy any food with salt substitute (potassium chloride).

COURT BOUILLON

2 onions, sliced
1 stalk celery, sliced
1 carrot, sliced
1 sprig of fresh dill
3 black peppercorns, crushed
2 cloves, crushed
1 bay leaf
1 cup water
1 cup white wine vinegar

1. Place all ingredients in a large stock pot and bring to a boil.
2. Reduce heat and cook at a low boil for 45 minutes.

Yield: 2 cups
5 Calories per cup
This bouillon is for poaching salmon, cod, or halibut. Any large pot with a rack will serve as a poacher.

FISH STOCK

3 pounds of fish heads and skeletons of sole, whiting or other white fish
2 onions, sliced
3 stalks of celery, sliced
1 carrot, sliced
½ cup fresh parsley, chopped
2 Tbsp. lemon juice
3 quarts water
¼ tsp. black pepper

1. Combine all ingredients in a large stock pot. Cover and bring to a full boil and reduce heat to medium simmer. Cook for 1 hour.
2. Strain.
3. Store in freezer or refrigerator.

Yield: 3 quarts
5 Calories per cup
This stock is to be used as a base for fish soups or stews.

appetizers

Cocktail parties are a popular way of entertaining, and wine and cheese has become almost standard at many of them. Be different. An array of some of our appetizers are far more interesting and far less caloric. Try them at your next party.

BAKED STUFFED CLAMS

(serves 6)

12 clams
2 Tbsp. onion, chopped fine
2 Tbsp. stock
4 Tbsp. seasoned bread crumbs
1 Tbsp. parsley
Black pepper to taste
2 Tbsp. Parmesan cheese

1. Steam clams until they open.
2. Remove from shells and chop fine.
3. Simmer onions in stock until tender.
4. Add bread crumbs, chopped clams and parsley to onions. Season with pepper. Sprinkle with Parmesan cheese.
5. Divide into 12 clam shells and bake in preheated 350° oven for 10 minutes.

45 Calories per serving

STUFFED EGGS

(serves 6)

6 eggs
¼ pound canned salmon
1 tsp. onion juice
1 tsp. lemon juice
1/8 tsp. black pepper, to taste
2 Tbsp. parsley, finely chopped

1. Hard boil eggs. Slice in half lengthwise. Remove yolks and discard.
2. Remove skin and bones of the salmon, and mash fine.

3. Add seasonings and mix well.
4. Place a little of the salmon mixture on each half of egg.
5. Sprinkle parsley on top.

50 Calories per serving

CLAM DIP

¼ pound clams, drained and minced
1 cup low-fat plain yogurt
1 tsp. lemon juice
¼ tsp. garlic powder
1/8 tsp. black pepper, to taste

1. Combine all ingredients.
2. Allow to stand for a couple of hours for spices to blend together.

210 Calories for recipe

COTTAGE CHEESE DIP

½ cup low-fat cottage cheese
1 tsp. cumin
1 tsp. curry powder
½ tsp. dill weed
1/8 tsp. black pepper

1. Beat cheese until smooth.
2. Add spices and allow to stand for several hours to enhance blend.

VARIATION: Blend in ½ cucumber from which seeds have been removed.

80 Calories for recipe
85 Calories for recipe with cucumber.

EGGPLANT STICKS

(serves 8)

1 eggplant (about 1 pound)
¼ cup skim milk
½ cup seasoned bread crumbs
1 tsp. oil

1. Wash eggplant.
2. Cut in half inch slices and then in sticks about ½-inch wide and ¼-inch thick.
3. Dip sticks in milk and then in bread crumbs.
4. Lightly grease baking pan and place sticks in it in a single layer.
5. Bake in a preheated 375° oven for 25-30 minutes or until soft inside and crisp outside.

45 Calories per serving

VARIATION: Zucchini sticks can be prepared the same way.

ROUMANIAN CHOPPED EGGPLANT

(serves 8)

1 eggplant (about 1 pound)
1 Tbsp. chopped onion
1 Tbsp. oil
2 Tbsp. tarragon or wine vinegar
½ tsp. oregano
¼ tsp. garlic powder
A pinch of crushed red pepper
1/8 tsp. ground black pepper, to taste

1. Place eggplant in a baking dish and slash each side with a knife to allow steam to escape.
2. Place under broiler for 20 minutes on each side or until the inside is very soft. The outside will blacken and the inside will remain light in color.
3. Remove from broiler. Cut eggplant in half and scoop out inside.
4. Chop insides with a pastry blender or chopping knife until no strings are left. DO NOT use a blender or food processor as the eggplant will become too mushy.
5. Add all ingredients to eggplant.
6. Mix well and refrigerate for at least 3-4 hours to allow spices to blend.

35 Calories per serving

FISH QUENNELLES

(serves 6)

½ pound any white fish, raw
2 egg whites
¼ cup matzoh meal
1/8 tsp. black pepper
1 cup fish stock

1. Place fish and egg whites in blender for a couple of minutes until you have a paste.
2. Add matzoh meal and pepper and mix together.
3. Form into small balls.
4. Bring stock to boiling point and drop balls into stock and cook for 10 minutes.
5. Remove carefully with a slotted spoon and cool. Refrigerate. Serve with horseradish sauce.

Sauce
1 Tbsp. yogurt
1 Tbsp. horseradish

Mix yogurt and horseradish together and allow to stand for one hour.

55 Calories per serving

HUMUS
(Mashed Chick Peas)

1 cup chick peas, cooked
1 Tbsp. sesame seeds
4 Tbsp. lemon juice
1 clove garlic, crushed
Fresh ground black pepper
Pasley sprigs and Paprika for garnish

Blend all ingredients in a food processor until you have a smooth paste.

Place in a serving dish and garnish with sprigs of parsley and a dash of paprika

35 Calories per Tbsp.

Serving Suggestion: Stuff stalks of celery with humus. One stalk has 5 calories.

MINIATURE MEXICAN MEATBALLS

(serves 6)

2 Tbsp. stock
2 cloves garlic, crushed
¼ cup onion, chopped fine
¼ green pepper, chopped fine
½ pound ground beef (very lean)
½ cup cooked brown rice
Freshly ground black pepper to taste
1/8 tsp. chili powder
½ cup cooked spinach, chopped and well
   drained
¼ cup chicken stock

1. Simmer onion, garlic and green pepper in stock until tender.
2. Combine all ingredients adding stock last. Mix together lightly.
3. Form into small rounds. Do not press together too tightly.
4. Place on a broiling rack to allow fat to drip down and bake in a preheated 375° oven for approximately 10-15 minutes.
5. Serve hot with parsley and cherry tomatoes for garnish. Makes about 24 meatballs.

25 Calories per meatball

STUFFED MUSHROOMS

(serves 6)

18 small to medium mushrooms
½ small onion, finely chopped
2 Tbsp. stock
6 mushroom stems, finely chopped
4 Tbsp. seasoned bread crumbs
1 Tbsp. parsley, chopped
2 Tbsp. stock

1. Snap off stems, leaving a small cavity for stuffing.
2. Simmer onions in stock until tender.
3. Add chopped mushroom stems and simmer 3 minutes longer.
4. Combine onions, mushrooms, bread crumbs and parsley. Mix well together.
5. Dip mushrooms in stock and stuff with a little bread crumb mixture.
6. Place in a baking dish and bake in a preheated 350° oven for 25-30 minutes.

30 Calories per serving

SPINACH STRUDLE

(serves 6)

Spinach stuffing
⅓ cup onion chopped fine
2 Tbsp. parsley, minced
¼ cup chicken stock
1 10-oz. package frozen spinach, chopped
¼ cup plain bread crumbs
1 egg white, slightly beaten
1 Tbsp. Parmesan cheese
¼ tsp. nutmeg
1/8 tsp. black pepper
4 strudle leaves or Phyllo leaves
2 Tbsp. skim milk
1 tsp. oil

1. Simmer onions and parsley in stock until tender.
2. Cook spinach, drain well and cool slightly.
3. Combine above ingredients and add bread crumbs, egg white, cheese, nutmeg and pepper. Mix well together.
4. Slightly dampen a towel.
5. Remove 2 strudle leaves from package and place them on top of towel.
6. Spread half of spinach misture along the narrow edge and roll up jelly-roll fashion.
7. Slash top in several places to allow steam to escape.
8. Brush top and sides with skim milk.
9. Grease baking pan and place strudle in pan.
10. Repeat above process with the next two strudle leaves. You must work quickly or leaves will dry up.
11. Bake in a preheated 400° oven for 25-30 minutes or until brown.
12. Divide each roll into six pieces.

70 Calories per serving

YOGURT VEGETABLE DIP

1 cup low-fat plain yogurt
2 Tbsp. dried vegetable flakes
1 tsp. fresh dill minced, or ½ tsp. dill weed
1 Tbsp. fresh parsley, chopped
Ground pepper to taste

Combine all ingredients and allow to stand for at least two hours to blend spices.

123 Calories for 1 cup.
8 Calories per Tbsp.

ZUCCHINI PIE

(serves 8)

2 cups zucchini, sliced thin
¼ cup stock or water
1½ cups skim milk
2 Tbsp. enriched white flour
2 egg whites, slightly beaten
2 oz. shredded cheese
1 tsp. caraway seeds

8" square pan, 2" high
1 tsp. oil

1. Simmer zucchini in stock or water until tender. Drain well.
2. Shake milk and flour vigorously in a jar. Pour into a bowl.
3. Add egg whites and mix well.
4. Add cheese and caraway seeds. Mix.
5. Grease pan and pour one-half milk-cheese mixture into it.
6. Distribute the zucchini in the pan.
7. Cover with remainder of milk-cheese mixture.
8. Bake in preheated 250° oven for 35-40 minutes or until a knife comes out clean. Serve immediately.

60 Calories for 1/8th pie.

soups

We have offered you about thirty soups—one for each day of the month. (A soup a day . . . keeps the hunger away!). We love soups because they are filling and satisfying. A steaming cup of soup on a cold day is as pleasurable as a crisp cold soup on a hot day. We have taken the mystery out of soup-making. Almost all of the ingredients can be combined and cooked at the same time. Most of us grew up having soups on special days, mostly holidays. With our quick preparation methods, soup can become part of your daily fare. The trick is in advance preparation; shop for all of your fresh vegetables at once and keep a supply of dried beans in the pantry. Don't throw away that turkey carcass, save it for making stock and freeze it for future use.

Once you have the soup habit, you will find it a most enjoyable part of your meal.

BEET BORSCHT

(serves 6)

1 pound beets, fresh or canned
1 cup beet juice
2 tsp. sugar
4 Tbsp. lemon juice
2 cups buttermilk

1. Cut ½ cup beets in strips and reserve.
2. Blend remaining beets with juices and buttermilk.
3. Add sugar and lemon juice and blend again.
4. Place a few strips of beets in each plate when serving.

If you use fresh beets, remove the green tops and cook them as you would spinach. Buy 1½ pounds of fresh beets to allow for the greens you are cutting off.

To cook fresh beets, cover with water and cook whole until tender. Remove skins.

This is a wonderful cold soup during the summer months. Add a small boiled potato and you have a meal.

70 Calories per serving

CABBAGE SOUP

(serves 12)

3 beef bones (optional)
8 cups stock
1½ pounds shredded cabbage
2 onions, chopped
1 pound canned tomatoes, chopped including
   liquid
1 medium potato, sliced thin
2 Tbsp. honey
2 Tbsp. red wine vinegar
3 Tbsp. lemon juice
½ tsp. black pepper
1 tsp. caraway seeds

Combine all ingredients and simmer for two hours. This soup improves with long slow cooking.

65 Calories per serving

CARROT RICE SOUP

(serves 8)

1 pound carrots
1 large onion
1 stalk celery
6 cups chicken stock
1 tsp. marjoram
1 tsp. fresh mint, chopped or ½ tsp. dried
½ cup cooked rice
¼ cup white wine
Black pepper to taste

1. Scrape carrots and cut into thin slices.
2. Chop onion and celery.
3. Simmer vegetables and spices in stock until tender.
4. Remove ½ cup carrots with a slotted spoon to reserve for garnish.
5. Cool soup and puree in a blender.
6. Place pureed soup back in saucepan, and add rice, wine and pepper.
7. Simmer slowly for 30 minutes. Garnish with the reserved carrots and a little fresh chopped mint when serving.

55 Calories per serving

CHICKEN SOUP

(serves 6)

6 cups water
1 3-pound chicken and giblets
2 carrots, scraped and quartered
2 onions, coarsely chopped
1 doz. sprigs parsley
6 sprigs fresh dill
2 stalks celery with leaves
1 parsnip
½ tsp. black pepper

1. Clean chicken and cut into quarters or eighths.
2. Place in a heavy covered saucepan with vegetables and water and simmer 1½ hours or until chicken is tender.
3. Skim off foam occasionally.
4. Cool and strain. Reserve vegetables for later use.
5. Refrigerate soup overnight, then skim off all fat.

25 Calories per serving of clear soup
Serving suggestions:
Cut up carrots and place some in soup with a little cooked onion.
Add some cooked rice.
Cook fine noodles and serve with soup.
Beat two egg whites and pour slowly into simmering soup for egg drop soup.
Use the chicken for any of our dishes that call for cooked chicken, such as the Rice Mold, Chicken Divan and Chicken Salad.

The vegetables can be combined with some chicken stock to make another soup. Just simmer the vegetables with 3 cups of stock for 10 minutes. Cool and puree in a blender. Add pepper to taste.

CHICKEN VEGETABLE SOUP

(serves 8)

6 cups water
2 pounds chicken backs and necks
4 fresh tomatoes
1 zucchini, chopped
2 onions, chopped
2 carrots, chopped
1 cup celery, chopped
½ cup string beans, cut in pieces
1 Tbsp. barley
½ tsp. black pepper
¼ tsp. paprika

1. Combine chicken and water and simmer 30 minutes. Skim off foam.
2. Add all vegetables, spices and barley and cook for 1 to 1½ hours.
3. Remove chicken parts.
4. Chill and then remove fat.
5. Heat to serve.

50 Calories per serving

VARIATION: For vegetarian vegetable soup eliminate the chicken parts and add another tablespoon of barley.

COLD CUCUMBER DILL SOUP

(serves 6)

2 large cucumbers
2 cups skim milk
1 cup low-fat cottage cheese
4 Tbsp. lemon juice
¼ cup fresh dill, chopped
1 sprig fresh parsley, chopped
2 Tbsp. fresh chives, minced
½ Tbsp. Dijon mustard

1. Peel cucumbers. Cut in half lengthwise and remove seeds.
2. Blend all ingredients together in a blender. Start at slow speed and increase to high after the first few minutes.
3. Refrigerate until thoroughly chilled.
4. Garnish with a bit of fresh dill and chives when serving.

70 Calories per serving

CORN SOUP

(serves 6)

1 cup celery, sliced
½ cup onion, chopped
2 cloves garlic, minced
2 cups chicken or vegetable stock
¼ tsp. pepper
2 cups creamed corn
2 Tbsp. parsley, chopped

1. Combine all ingredients except corn and simmer 15 minutes.
2. Add corn to simmering stock and continue to cook for 15 minutes more.
3. Garnish soup with fresh parsley when serving.

75 Calories per 6 oz. serving

If you use fresh corn or corn kernels, puree in blender with a little stock.

CREAM OF CABBAGE SOUP

(serves 6)

1 pound cabbage, shredded
1 medium potato, sliced thin
4 cups vegetable or chicken stock
½ tsp. dill weed
1 tsp. caraway seeds
1 cup evaporated skim milk
1/8 tsp. freshly ground white pepper to taste
Grated raw carrot

1. Simmer cabbage and potato in stock until vegetables are tender.
2. Cool and blend into a puree. Return to saucepan.
3. Add spices and evaporated milk.
4. Simmer slowly for 15 minutes. Adjust seasonings.
5. Garnish with a little grated carrot when serving.

70 Calories per serving.

This can be made with plain skim milk for 55 calories per serving.

CREAM OF TOMATO SOUP

(serves 6)

1 cup water or stock
1 onion, chopped
1 stalk celery, chopped, including leaves
1 1-pound can tomato puree
½ tsp. thyme
1 Tbsp. fresh basil or 1 tsp. dried
1/8 tsp. black pepper
2 cups skim milk
2 Tbsp. flour

1. Simmer onions and celery until tender.
2. Add tomatoes and spices and simmer 45 minutes.
3. Cool and puree in blender. Return to saucepan and heat.
4. Combine flour and milk in a jar and shake vigorously.
5. Add slowly to hot soup.
6. Simmer on a low flame until the soup comes to the boiling point. Do not boil.

90 Calories per serving

CUCUMBER SOUP

(serves 6)

2 cucumbers (about 1 pound)
1 qt. low-fat buttermilk
1 Tbsp. green onion, chopped
¼ cup fresh parsley, chopped
¼ tsp. black pepper
¼ tsp. dill seed for soup
¼ tsp. dill seed for garnish

1. Peel cucumbers. Cut in half lengthwise and remove seeds. Grate or chop in food processor.
2. Combine cucumber with all ingredients.
3. Chill for at least two hours to allow the spices to blend.
4. Serve cold. Garnish with the dill seed and a little chopped parsley.

95 Calories per serving

FRUIT SOUP

(serves 6)

1 pound fresh peaches
¼ qt. fresh strawberries
1 cup cooking liquid from peaches
3 cups buttermilk
¼ tsp. cinnamon
¼ tsp. vanilla
6 strawberries, sliced, for garnish
dash nutmeg

1. Cook peaches. Remove skin and pits.
2. Hull strawberries.
3. Combine all ingredients in a blender and whip until smooth.
4. Garnish with sliced strawberries. Sprinkle with a little nutmeg.

90 Calories per serving

MANCHU CHICKEN MUSHROOM SOUP

(serves 6)

1½ qts. chicken consomme
10 oz. fresh mushrooms
6 leaves Romaine lettuce

1. Heat consomme to a boil.
2. Wash drain and thinly slice mushrooms. Add to soup.
3. Wash, dry and tear each piece of lettuce into thirds.
4. Place three pieces of lettuce in each bowl at the moment of serving. The lettuce should float on top and remain crisp.

35 Calories per serving

TOMATO-CELERY SOUP

(serves 6)

1 16-oz. can crushed tomatoes
3 cups chicken stock
2 cups celery, sliced in small pieces
1 onion, chopped
2 Tbsp. raw brown rice
½ tsp. thyme
3 cloves garlic, crushed
1 tsp. sugar
½ tsp. celery seed
Black pepper to taste

1. Combine all ingredients in a heavy covered pot.
2. Simmer for 1 hour.

60 Calories per serving

salads

Salads are a favorite with us. They are colorful, attractive, full of vitamins, minerals and fiber and can be used as an accompaniment to a meal or as a main dish.

Salads are filling and most vegetables used in salads are low in calories. One pound of lettuce is worth about 50 calories, so use it at least once and preferably twice a day.

Be experimental with salad ingredients and combinations. Try some of the following:

Salad greens: arugala, Boston lettuce, chicory, endive, escarole, red leaf lettuce, Romaine lettuce and spinach leaves.

Raw vegetables: broccoli, regular cauliflower, Jerusalem artichokes (difficult to find in local supermarkets), mushrooms, onions, parsley, peppers, radishes, tomatoes, turnip and watercress.

Mix them together for a light salad. Add fruit, cooked vegetables or protein foods for combinations as exciting as your imagination can make them.

THREE BEAN SALAD

(serves 8)

1 cup kidney beans, cooked
1 cup string beans, cooked
1 cup garbanzo beans, cooked
1 large red onion, sliced in rings

Combine all beans and marinate in vinaigrette dressing overnight (see SALAD DRESSINGS).

80 Calories per serving

CAULIFLOWER-ALMOND SALAD

(serves 8)

3 cups cauliflower flowerettes
2 Tbsp. slivered almonds (½ oz.)
2 Tbsp. carrots, grated

1. Steam cauliflower until tender, but not soft.
2. Toss with vinaigrette dressing (see SALAD DRESSINGS).
3. Garnish with slivered almonds and carrots.

30 Calories per serving

CHICKEN SALAD

(serves 6)

2 cups cooked chicken, cubed
1 cup celery, chopped
1 apple cut in cubes
1 cup mandarin oranges
2 Tbsp. parsley
1 tsp. fresh ginger, chopped
1/8 tsp. black pepper

1. Combine all ingredients.
2. Toss with yogurt dressing. (see SALAD DRESSINGS).

195 Calories per serving without dressing.

COLE SLAW

(serves 6)

3 cups cabbage, shredded
2 carrots, cleaned and shredded
3 Tbsp. scallions, chopped
1 Tbsp. chives
¼ tsp. freshly ground black pepper
2 Tbsp. mayonnaise
6 Tbsp. yogurt
2 Tbsp. lemon juice
2 Tbsp. parsley, chopped, for garnish

1. Toss all vegetables together.
2. Combine mayonnaise, yogurt and lemon juice.
3. Pour over vegetables. Mix well and let stand for at least 2 hours.
4. Garnish with parsley.

25 Calories per serving without dressing
60 Calories per serving with dressing

VARIATIONS: Add 1 cup chopped celery
Sprinkle with chopped fresh tarragon

PINEAPPLE COLE SLAW

(serves 6)

3 cups cabbage, shredded
1 cup mixed red and green pepper, chopped
1 cup low-fat plain yogurt
¼ cup pineapple juice, unsweetened
1 tsp. chopped mint
1 cup pineapple chunks, canned in its own juice
1/8 tsp. ground pepper to taste

1. Place cabbage and mixed peppers in a bowl.
2. Combine yogurt, pineapple juice and mint.
3. Pour over cole slaw and mix well. Allow to stand for 2 hours.
4. Add pineapple chunks, toss and season with pepper.

60 Calories per serving

CUCUMBER BOATS STUFFED WITH TUNA SALAD

(serves 6)

3 cucumbers
7 oz. can tuna, water pack
4 oz. low-fat cottage cheese
2 oz. crushed pineapple
1 Tbsp. parsley, chopped
1 Tbsp. chives, minced
1/8 tsp. black pepper

1. Cut cucumbers in half lengthwise. Remove seeds and pat dry.
2. Drain tuna.
3. Add remaining ingredients and mix together very well. Season to taste.
4. Stuff cucumber boats.
5. Serve on a lettuce bed. Garnish with cherry tomatoes, watercress and a slice of lime.

80 Calories per serving

FRUIT AND VEGETABLE SALAD

(serves 6)

3 oranges
2 apples
2 bananas
2 Tbsp. lime juice
1 cup beets, drained and sliced
Lettuce

1. Peel and cut oranges into rounds.
2. Cut apples into thin wedges. Do not peel.
3. Slice bananas in lengthwise wedges.
4. Pour lime juice over apples, bananas and oranges to keep them from darkening. Arrange fruit and beets attractively on plate over a lettuce bed.

Dressing
½ cup low-fat yogurt
1 Tbsp. lime juice
1 Tbsp. honey
2 Tbsp. beet juice

5. Combine yogurt with juices and honey and pour over salad.

130 Calories for salad and 2 Tbsp. dressing

GREEN SALAD

(serves 6)

1½ pounds varied types of lettuce

Wash, spin dry or dry with paper towels. Shred into bite-size pieces. Toss with any of our salad dressings.

15 Calories for 1/6th recipe

MACARONI SALAD

(serves 6)

3 cups cooked macaroni
1 cup celery, chopped
½ cup green pepper, chopped
2 Tbsp. parsley, chopped
1 Tbsp. celery seed
1/8 tsp. fresh ground pepper
1 cup tarragon-tomato dressing (see SALAD DRESSINGS)

1. Combine macaroni, vegetables and seasonings.
2. Toss with tarragon-tomato dressing.

115 Calories per serving

MOLDED FRUIT AND VEGETABLE SALAD

(serves 6)

1 cup celery, chopped
2 carrots, shredded
½ cup peas, cooked
1 red pepper, chopped
½ cup crushed pineapple canned in its own juice
1 Tbsp. unflavored gelatin
1 cup orange juice, unsweetened
2 Tbsp. lime juice

1 qt. mold

1. Combine all vegetables and pineapple in a bowl.
2. Sprinkle gelatin over ½ cup pineapple juice.
3. Heat until gelatin is dissolved and add remaining juices.
4. Pour over vegetables and mix well.
5. Rinse mold in ice cold water. Pour vegetable-gelatin mixture into mold and chill overnight.
6. Unmold on a lettuce bed.

95 Calories per serving

PITA POCKETS SALAD

(serves 6)

6 small whole wheat pitas
2 7-oz. cans tuna, water pack
½ cup celery, chopped
2 Tbsp. parsley, minced
½ cup low-fat yogurt
2 Tbsp. lemon juice
Black pepper
½ head lettuce, shredded
1 cucumber, thinly sliced
2 tomatoes, thinly sliced
2 Tbsp. mung bean sprouts

1. Drain tuna and chop fine.
2. Combine tuna with celery, parsley, yogurt, lemon juice and pepper.
3. Fill the pita pocket with tuna.
4. Top with as many of the salad ingredients as will fit into pocket.

115 Calories per serving
80 Calories per pita

POTATO SALAD

(serves 8)

3 cups cooked potatoes, cubed (about 1½ pound)
½ cup green pepper, chopped
1 Tbsp. celery seed
2 Tbsp. parsley, chopped
2 Tbsp. mayonnaise
½ cup low-fat plain yogurt
1 Tbsp. onion juice
2 Tbsp. fresh parsley, minced, for garnish
2 Tbsp. grated carrot for garnish

1. Combine all vegetables in a bowl.
2. Mix yogurt, mayonnaise and seasonings.
3. Pour over salad and mix well.
4. Garnish with parsley and carrot when serving.

95 Calories per serving

RATATOUILLE

(serves 12)

3 cloves garlic, crushed
1 large onion, chopped
1 green pepper, chopped
½ cup stock
2 zucchini (about 1 pound)
1 small eggplant (about 2 pounds)
5 very ripe tomatoes (about 2 pounds)
2 Tbsp. fresh basil or 1 Tbsp. dried
3 Tbsp. parsley, chopped
¼ tsp. black pepper freshly ground
½ pound mushrooms, sliced

1. In a large saucepan, simmer garlic, onions and green pepper in stock until slightly softened.
2. Slice zucchini.
3. Peel eggplant and cut into cubes.
4. Cut tomatoes into cubes.
5. Add vegetables, herbs and spices and continue simmering on a low flame for 45 minutes, mixing occasionally.
6. Add mushrooms and simmer for another 15 minutes or until all vegetables are soft and blended together.

55 Caloiries per serving

This can be used as an appetizer, served cold, as a side dish or as a main dish when topped with some grated cheese and bread crumbs.

RICE SALAD

(serves 6)

2 cups cooked brown rice
¼ cup stock or water
1 cup onion, chopped
2 cups fresh tomatoes, chopped
½ cup green pepper, chopped
¼ cup fresh parsley, chopped
1 Tbsp. oil
1 Tbsp. chives or 1 tsp. dried
1 Tbsp. fresh dil or 1 tsp. dried
¼ tsp. black pepper

Cucumber slices and Radish roses for garnish

1. Cool rice.
2. Simmer onion in stock until transparent and cool.
3. Combine all ingredients and seasonings.
4. Shape into an oval mound on large platter. Cover with plastic wrap and chill several hours.
5. Garnish with cucumber slices and radish roses.

115 Calories per serving

VEGETABLES IN MARINADE

1 cup water
½ cup white wine
1 Tbsp. lemon juice
1 Tbsp. sugar
½ tsp. oregano
¼ tsp. black pepper
1 Tbsp. dried parsley
½ tsp. garlic powder
2 carrots, chopped
2 stalks celery, chopped
1 green pepper, chopped
1 sweet red pepper, chopped
½ head white cauliflower, cut in flowerets
½ pound fresh mushrooms, sliced

1. Combine all ingredients except vegetables and bring to a slow boil.
2. Lower heat and add vegetables.
3. Simmer for *5 minutes only*. Do not allow vegetables to get soft.
4. Cool and then refrigerate overnight.

60 Calories for recipe
To serve as an appetizer or for salad, drain the vegetables and use accordingly.

STUFFED YELLOW SQUASH BOATS

(serves 6)

3 small yellow squash
1 pound low-fat cottage cheese
3 scallions, chopped
1 tsp. marjoram
1 Tbsp. poppy seeds
Pepper to taste
Pimento slices

1. Simmer squash about 10 minutes and cool.
2. Cut off ends and slice in half lengthwise. Scoop out insides leaving ¼-inch of shell. Cool.
3. Mix cheese and squash.
4. Add remaining ingredients and mix well.
5. Stuff shells and chill.
6. Garnish with pimento.

85 Calories per serving

TABBOULEH

(serves 6)

1 cup cracked wheat (Bulgur)
4 scallions, choipped
1 cup fresh parsley, chopped
3 Tbsp. fresh mint, chopped or 1 Tbsp. dried
1/8 tsp. black pepper
1 cucumber, chopped
2 tomatoes, cubed
1 Tbsp. oil
2 Tbsp. lemon juice
1/8 tsp. black pepper
1 clove garlic, crushed

1. Wash and drain the cracked wheat.
2. Cover with boiling water and let the cracked wheat soak for one hour.
3. Drain well and pat dry with paper towels.
4. Combine wheat, scallions, parsley and spices. Allow to stand together for several hours.
5. Just before serving, add cucumbers and tomatoes.
6. Add oil, lemon juice, pepper and garlic and toss well.
7. Serve chilled.

110 Calories per serving

TOMATO ASPIC VEGETABLE SALAD

(serves 6)

3 cups tomato juice (salt-free)
1 Tbsp. unflavored gelatin (1 packet)
1 Tbsp. onion juice
¼ cup white wine
2 Tbsp. lemon juice
1/8 tsp. fresh ground pepper
1 yellow squash, thinly sliced (about ½ pound)
½ pound mushrooms, sliced
½ cup celery, chopped
¼ cup red onion, thinly sliced
1½ qt. mold
Lettuce leaves

1. Sprinkle unflavored gelatin over ½ cup tomato juice and heat until gelatin dissolves.
2. Add onion juice, white wine, lemon juice and pepper.
3. Simmer squash and zucchini in a little water for 5 minutes.
4. Combine all vegetables in a bowl.
5. Add gelatin mix.
6. Rinse mold in ice cold water and pour gelatin and vegetables into it.
7. Chill overnight and unmold on a lettuce bed when ready to serve.

70 Calories per serving

TOMATOES STUFFED WITH VEGETABLE COTTAGE CHEESE

(serves 6)

3 radishes, chopped
1 cucumber, chopped
6 scallions, chopped
1 red pepper, chopped
1 pound low-fat cottage cheese
½ cup low-fat plain yogurt
1/8 tsp. black pepper
6 tomatoes (about 2 pounds)
Paprika
2 Tbsp. parsley, finely chopped
Lettuce leaves

1. Combine all vegetables (except tomatoes) with yogurt and cottage cheese and add black pepper.
2. Cut thin slice of blossom end of tomato and cut tomatoes tulip fashion, zig-zagging the top. Do not cut through. Scoop out centers.
3. Spread tomato apart and stuff with cottage cheese.
4. Sprinkle with paprika and parsley.
5. Serve on a lettuce bed.

120 Calories per serving

TUNA MOLD

(serves 6)

1 small onion, finely chopped
2 celery stalks, finely chopped
½ green pepper, finely chopped
2 Tbsp. parsley, finely chopped
½ cup water chestnuts, finely chopped
2 7-oz. cans tuna, water pack
½ cup fat-free plain yogurt
1 tsp. Worcestershire sauce
2 Tbsp. lemon juice
1/8 tsp. black pepper
1 Tbsp. gelatin (1 packet)
½ cup dry sherry
1 cup hot chicken stock

1 qt. mold

1. Flake tuna.
2. Mix tuna and chopped vegetables.
3. Add lemon juice and spices to yogurt.
4. Mix yogurt dressing with tuna and vegetables and mix well.
5. Sprinkle gelatin over sherry.
6. Add hot chicken stock, stirring until gelatin is dissolved.
7. Add to tuna-vegetable mixture.
8. Rinse mold and add in all ingredients.
9. Refrigerate several hours until set.
10. When ready to serve, unmold on a bed or lettuce and garnish with cherry tomatoes.

140 Calories per serving.

TURKEY ASPIC

(serves 6)

1 Tbsp. unflavored gelatin (1 packet)
½ cup unsweetened pineapple juice
2 cups white turkey meat
½ cup peas, cooked and cooled
1 cup celery, chopped
½ cup red pepper, chopped
½ cup crushed pineapple in its own juice
1 tsp. curry powder
½ tsp. cumin
1/8 tsp. black pepper

1 qt. mold

1. Sprinkle gelatin over juice and heat until gelatin is dissolved.
2. Combine remaining ingredients and add gelatin mixture. Mix well.
3. Rinse mold with cold water. Pour turkey-vegetable mixture into the mold. Refrigerate for several hours until set.
4. Unmold on a lettuce bed. Garnish with cherry tomatoes.

215 Calories per serving

TURNIP AND CARROT SALAD

(serves 6)

1 turnip, shredded
2 carrots, shredded
Vinaigrette dressing (see SALAD DRESSINGS)
1/8 tsp. black pepper to taste
½ cup alfalfa sprouts

1. Combine carrots and turnips.
2. Toss with dressing and season to taste.
3. Top with sprouts.

25 Calories per serving

main dishes

Main Dishes, by definition, are the focal point of every meal. The ingredients in the main dish sets the pace for the remainder of the meal. This section contains a wide variety of delectable choices: Fruited Chicken, Chicken Kiev and Chicken in Wine, to name a few of the most popular dishes. Chili Con Carne, Cioppino, Fish Au Gratin, Meatless Lasagna, Stuffed Cabbage and Turkey Divan are a few of the other highlights in the Main Dishes.

All of these recipes can be featured for lunch, brunch, dinner, late supper, buffet parties and even for breakfasts. All are nutritionally balanced, calorie controlled and delightfully seasoned.

Any one of a number of appetizers, soups, salads and desserts can be artfully added to round out a full course nutritionally balanced meal. Refer to your calorie count, stay within the limits you have set for yourself and prepare to feast where you might have had to fast.

ARGENTINE FRUITED CHICKEN

(serves 8)

1½ pounds chicken cutlets
2 onions, sliced
2 Tbsp. stock
1 Tbsp. fresh parsley, chopped
1 stalk celery, sliced
1 yellow or green squash, cubed
2 medium white potatoes, peeled and thinly sliced
2 small sweet potatoes, peeled and cubed (about ½ pound)
2 medium apples, unpeeled and cut into 16ths
2 large pears, unpeeled and cut into 16ths
¼ cup raisins
½ tsp. thyme
1 bay leaf
½ tsp. black pepper
½ cup tomato sauce
½ cup white wine
2 cups stock

1. Trim chicken cutlets and cut into 2" pieces. Set aside to be added later.
2. Combine remainder of ingredients in a large heavy covered pot.
3. Bring to a low boil.
4. Lower heat and simmer for 20 minutes.
5. Add chicken pieces and continue cooking for 10 minutes or until vegetables are tender, not mushy.

Fruits and vegetables may be substituted regionally and seasonally.

250 Calories per serving

BAKED ITALIAN CHICKEN

(serves 6)

2½ to 3-pound young chicken

1. Trim off visible fat and extra skin.
2. Cut into 16 serving portions.
3. Place in heated pan with no fat.
4. Brown over high heat to render off as much fat as possible from skin.
5. Arrange chicken pieces in large flat baking pan.

Sauce
1 large onion, cut into thin rings
4 Tbsp. water or stock
8 oz. can tomato sauce
½ cup sweet wine
½ tsp. basil
½ tsp. organo

¼ tsp. peppet
1 bay leaf

1. Brown onions in water or stock.
2. Add all ingredients to browned onion rings and simmer together for 10 minutes.
3. Pour sauce over chicken.
4. Bake for 1 hour in preheated 350° oven.
5. Chill several hours and then remove all fat.

175 Calories per serving

BREAST OF CURRY CHICKEN

(serves 6)

1½ pound chicken cutlets, cut into 12 serving size pieces
¼ tsp. paprika
2 large cloves garlic, minced
1 medium onion, cut into rings
½ cup stock
1 cup mushrooms, sliced
1 small apple, skinned and grated
1 tsp. curry powder
¼ tsp. cumin
¼ cup raisins
6 lemon slices, cut in half

1. Remove all visible fat from chicken. Sprinkle with paprika, set aside.
2. Simmer garlic and onions in stock until transparent.
3. Add mushrooms and apple and simmer for 5 minutes.

4. Add curry powder, cumin, raisins and lemon slices and simmer 10 minutes, stirring occasionally.
5. Place chicken breasts in large flat baking pan. Pour sauce over all, placing ½ lemon slice on each fillet.
6. Bake in preheated 350° oven for 30 minutes.
7. Place under broiler flame for 3 minutes just before serving, to brown tops.
   May be served over brown rice bed.

220 Calories per serving

NOTE: May be prepared with turkey cutlets; fish fillets (reduce calories by 50 if fish is used); veal cutlets.

CHEESE OMELET

(serves 1)

1 whole egg
2 Tbsp. skim milk
1 tsp. butter or margarine
2 Tbsp. low-fat cottage cheese
Dash of black pepper

1. Whisk egg and milk.
2. Heat pan until a drop of water sizzles. Add butter and heat again.
3. Pour egg mixture into heated pan.
4. Allow to just set.
5. Place cheese on one half of omelet. Fold over and cover. Reduce heat. Cook 3 minutes.
6. Sprinkle with black pepper and serve.

100 Calories for omelet
35 Calories for butter

CHICKEN KIEV

(serves 6)

1½ pounds chicken cutlets, all fat removed
2 Tbsp. sweet whipped butter
¼ cup skim evaporated milk
1 Tbsp. lemon juice
2 Tbsp. dried chives, snipped
¼ tsp. black pepper
3 Tbsp. skim milk
¼ cup seasoned bread crumbs
2 Tbsp. flour
1 Tbsp. oil
Cherry tomatoes
Fresh parsley sprigs

1. Divide chicken into 6 portions and pat dry. Create a pocked in each fillet by slicing almost all the way through.
2. Add skim milk to softened, not melted butter.
3. Add the lemon juice, chives and black pepper and mix.
4. Shape butter mixture in wax paper to form a square and place in freezer. Freeze until firm.
5. When firm enough to work with, slice into six sticks.
6. Place one butter stick in pocket of each chicken fillet and press together to seal.
7. Combine flour and bread crumbs.
8. Dip fillet in skim milk and then in flour-crumb mixture. Coat lightly.
9. Heat pan until a drop of water sizzles. Add oil and heat again. Brown chicken lightly on both sides. Do not cook through.
10. Just before serving, place chicken in baking pan and bake in preheated 400° oven for 20 minutes.
11. Garnish with cherry tomatoes and parsley.

240 Calories per serving

CHICKEN MARENGO

(serves 6)

1 3-pound chicken, cut into 12 pieces
3 small potatoes, sliced very thin
3 small onions, cut into quarters
4 medium fresh tomatoes, cut into quarters
10 oz. mushrooms, sliced
2 cloves garlic, minced
2 cups stock
½ cup sweet red wine
½ tsp. thyme
¼ tsp. black pepper
¼ tsp. sage

1. Remove all visible fat on chicken.
2. Heat pan to very high heat and brown chicken quickly on all sides to render off as much fat as possible.
3. Set aside to drain on paper towels.
4. Place vegetables and stock in a heavy pot and bring to a boil.
5. Turn heat down and add seasonings, wine and chicken pieces.
6. Cook for 20 minutes or until chicken is tender and potatoes are soft.
7. Chill and then remove all fat.
8. Heat before serving.

220 Calories per serving

CHICKEN RICE MOLD

(serves 8)

3 cups cooked converted rice
2 cups cooked cubed chicken
1 cup cooked green peas
2 fresh peaches cut into cubes
¼ cup chicken broth
1 tsp. Worcestershire sauce
1/8 tsp. black pepper

1. Combine all ingredients in a large bowl.
2. Place in a covered 1½ quart mold. Ring-shaped is best for this recipe.
3. Refrigerate overnight to be sure it is firm.
4. Unmold and garnish with cherry tomatoes, radish roases, cucumber slices or unmold onto a bed of greens.

NOTE: This is a great way to use up the chicken after making chicken soup, or 1 pound of chicken cutlets can be simmered in stock for 15 minutes if you prefer all white meat. Nice dish for summer meals and for buffet entertaining. You may substitute turkey for chicken... and canned peach halves for fresh, providing the can is packed in its own juice.

225 Calories per serving

CHICKEN VERMOUTH

(serves 6)

1½ pounds chicken cutlets
3 Tbsp. skim milk
¼ cup seasoned bread crumbs
1 Tbsp. oil for frying

1. Cut, trim and divide cutlets into 12 serving pieces.
2. Dip in skim milk.
3. Dip in bread crumbs. Fry in 1 Tbsp. oil until golden brown on both sides.
4. Arrange in baking casserole.

Sauce
½ cup chicken stock
½ cup dry vermouth
2 Tbsp. fresh parsley, chopped
½ cup water chestnuts
1/8 tsp. black pepper

1. Combine all ingredients and simmer for 10 minutes.
2. Pour sauce over chicken and bake for 30 minutes in preheated 350° oven.

200 Calories per serving

NOTE: May be prepared with turkey cutlets; fish fillets (reduce calories by 50 if using fish); veal cutlets.

CHICKEN WITH RICE AND PEAS

(serves 6)

2 cups basic medium white sauce (see BASIC SAUCES)
½ pound fresh mushrooms
1 Tbsp. dried chives
½ tsp. black pepper
2 oz. grated Swiss cheese
2 Tbsp. sweet red pepper, chopped, or strips of pimento, sliced
2 Tbsp. fresh parsley
½ cup fresh or frozen green peas
3 cups leftover cooked diced chicken
1 cup cooked brown rice
1 fresh tomato, cut into thin slices

1. Heat sauce to desired thickness.
2. Add mushrooms, chives, pepper, cheese, red pepper and parsley and cook for 10 minutes.
3. Add peas and chicken to sauce and cook for 5 minutes.
4. Arrange cooked rice along bottom and up sides of baking pan.
5. Pour chicken, peas, cheese sauce mixture over rice. Arrange fresh tomato slices over all.
6. Bake in preheated 350° oven for 20 minutes.

265 Calories per serving

CHILI CON POCO CARNE

(serves 6)

1 pound lean round beef, ground
3 medium onions, chopped
¼ cup stock or water
1 1-pound can tomato puree
3 tsp. chili powder
¼ tsp. black pepper
1 tsp. oregano
1 1-pound can red kidney beans or 2 cups of
    cooked red kidney beans

1. Render fat from meat in large pan, drain and discard fat. Set aside.
2. Brown onions in stock, using same pan.
3. Add puree, chili powder, black pepper and oregano.
4. Discard one half of the liquid in bean can and add remaining half to simmering sauce.
5. Add one half the beans to the sauce.
6. Mash remaining half of beans with fork in flat dish and add to simmering chili.
7. Add meat and simmer 30 minutes on medium flame.

305 Calories per serving

CIOPPINO

(serves 6)

1 cup onion, chopped
1 green pepper, chopped
½ cup parsley, chopped
4 cloves garlic, minced
½ cup stock
1 1-pound can tomatoes
1 bay leaf
¼ tsp. thyme
¼ tsp. marjoram
½ tsp. Tabasco
1/8 tsp. black pepper
½ cup dry white wine
1 pound halibut, cut in cubes
½ pound scallops

1. Simmer onion, green pepper, parsley and garlic in the stock until tender.
2. Add tomatoes and spices. Simmer for 2 hours, stirring occasionally.
3. Add wine. Cook 20 minutes more.
4. Add halibut. Simmer 10 minutes.
5. Add scallops. Simmer 5 minutes more.

150 Calories per serving

COQ AU VIN (CHICKEN IN WINE)

(serves 6)

1½ pounds chicken cutlets
2 Tbsp. plain bread crumbs
2 Tbsp. skim milk
1 Tbsp. oil
2 medium onions, chopped
4 Tbsp. stock
1 large green pepper, chopped
2 fresh tomatoes, chopped
1 cup chicken stock
½ cup dry white wine
¼ tsp. black pepper
¼ tsp. garlic powder
2 cups cooked brown rice

1. Cut, trim and divide chicken into 12 pieces.
2. Dip the pieces in skim milk.
3. Lightly coat with bread crumbs.
4. Fry in heated pan with oil until golden brown on both sides and then arrange in large flat casserole.
5. Cook onions in 4 Tbsp. stock until golden brown.
6. Add green pepper until tender.
7. Add fresh tomatoes and simmer 5 minutes, adding more stock or water if necessary.
8. Add 1 cup chicken stock, wine, pepper and garlic powder and cook together 5 minutes.
9. Puree in blender.
10. Pour sauce over chicken fillets in casserole and bake in preheated 350° oven, covered with foil, for 20 minutes.
11. Uncover and bake 15 minutes longer.
12. Serve over a bed of brown rice.

270 Calories per serving of 2 fillets

EGGPLANT PARMIGIANA

(serves 6)

2 medium sized eggplants (1 pound each)
¼ cup skim milk
½ cup seasoned bread crumbs
1 tsp. oil

1. Wash eggplants but do not peel. Slice into 12 ¼-inch slices each, for a total of 24 slices.
2. Dip slices in skim milk.
3. Lightly coat with bread crumbs.
4. Lightly oil a cookie sheet and heat in oven.
5. Place eggplant slices on heated pan and bake in preheated 400° oven for at least 20 minutes, or until golden brown and tender . . . not crisp. Set aside.

Sauce
1 6-oz. can tomato paste
1 28-oz. can crushed tomatoes in puree
2 Tbsp. red wine vinegar
½ tsp. garlic powder
1 tsp. sugar
1 tsp. oregano
1 tsp. basil

1 tsp. dried parsley
1/8 tsp. black pepper, coarse ground

1. Combine all sauce ingredients in large pan and cook at low simmer for 30 minutes.
2. Spread a small amount of sauce along bottom and sides of large baking casserole.
3. Arrange a layer of 12 slices of eggplant and pour half the sauce to cover all.
4. Repeat, ending with sauce.

Topping
½ pound whey cheese (fat-free cottage cheese may be substituted
1 egg white

2 Tbsp. seasoned bread crumbs
2 Tbsp. Parmesan cheese

1. Mix cheese, egg white and bread crumbs together to form firm topping for eggplant.
2. Drop by spoonfuls over each slice.
3. Bake in preheated 350° oven for 30 minutes.
   Sprinkle with Parmesan cheese just before serving.

170 Calories per serving

FAST FLOUNDER-ASPARAGUS CASSEROLE

(serves 6)

1½ pounds flounder fillets divided into 12 portions
1 Tbsp. lemon juice
2 packages of frozen asparagus spears approx. 10 oz. each, or 12 fresh stalks in season
1 cup basic thick white sauce (see BASIC SAUCES)
1 tsp. curry powder
1/8 tsp. coarsely ground black pepper
2 oz. cheddar cheese, shredded
¼ tsp. oil

1. Drain fish, pat dry and place on paper towels to drain further.
2. Sprinkle lemon juice over fish.
3. Cook asparagus 4 minutes and remove from pan while still firm and green. Drain and dry on paper towel.

4. Heat sauce with curry, pepper and cheese. Do not boil, but cheese should be melted and blended into sauce.
5. Oil casserole with the ¼ tsp. oil.
6. Arrange asparagus along bottom and up sides of round of oval casserole.
7. Place fish fillets on top of asparagus and pour cheese sauce over all.
8. Bake in preheated 350° oven about 30 minutes or until bubbled and fish appears white.
9. Place under broiler for 3 minutes if brown top is desired.

170 Calories per serving

FISH AU GRATIN

(serves 6)

1 pound fillet of flounder, sole or other thin white fish
1 cup basic thick white sauce (see BASIC SAUCES)
2 oz. Swiss cheese
1/8 tsp. black pepper
½ pound red salmon
4 potato chips

1. Drain fish, pat dry and dry further on paper towels.
2. Heat white sauce with cheese and pepper to desired thickness.
3. Lightly oil bottom of a casserole and place fish fillets along bottom of pan.
4. Top off each fillet with a strip of the fresh red salmon.
5. Pour cheese sauce over all.
6. Crush potato chips between waxed paper layers and sprinkle over top of casserole.
7. Bake in preheated 400° oven for 15 minutes or until fish is firm and white.

200 Calories per serving

FISH DINNER IN A DISH

(serves 6)

1½ pounds flounder fillets
1 Tbsp. lemon juice
2 Tbsp. water
1 onion, sliced into thin rings
1 small tomato, thinly sliced
3 small potatoes, thinly sliced
1/8 tsp. black pepper

1. Divide fillets into 12 portions.
2. Drain, pat dry and place on paper towel to dry further.
3. Sprinkle with lemon juice.
4. Place 2 Tbsp. water in bottom of baking dish and arrange onion rings, tomato slices and potatoes alternately along bottom of pan.
5. Sprinkle with black pepper to taste and bake for 20 minutes in preheated 400° oven.
6. Remove from oven and then arrange fish fillets to cover all the vegetables.

Topping
2 Tbsp. mayonnaise
2 Tbsp. seasoned bread crumbs
1 Tbsp. parsley, chopped
Paprika for garnish

1. Combine all topping ingredients and mix well.
2. Spread topping over all pieces of fish, covering all edges.
3. Sprinkle very lightly with paprika, return to oven and bake 10-15 minutes or until fish is snow white and flaky. Serve immediately from casserole so that fish does not come apart.

185 Calories per serving of 2 fillet pieces

FISH TANDOORI

(serves 6)

1½ pounds fish fillets
¼ tsp. oil

Sauce
½ cup low-fat plain yogurt
¼ tsp. ginger
¼ tsp. cinnamon
1 tsp. curry powder
¼ tsp. cumin
¼ tsp. white pepper
¼ tsp. garlic powder

1. Drain, pat dry and then dry further on paper towels.
2. Arrange fillets in slightly oiled pan.
3. Combine all sauce ingredients, mix well and let stand in refrigerator 1 hour or longer.
4. Brush sauce over fillets, covering carefully.
5. Bake 10-15 minutes in preheated 400° oven.
6. Place under broiler for 3 minutes if browning is desired.

110 Calories per serving

FLAMED VEAL WITH COGNAC AND GRAPES

(serves 6)

3 Tbsp. pancake flour
2 Tbsp. skim milk
1½ pounds veal, sliced into 12 very thin pieces
1 Tbsp. oil
10 oz. fresh mushrooms, sliced
½ cup dry white wine
1 tsp. thyme
1/8 tsp. black pepper
1 cup white grapes
4 Tbsp. cognac

1. Make paste of flour and milk.
2. Cover each piece of veal with a light coating of the pancake flour and milk batter, using fingers, or a kitchen knife to help spread it around each piece.
3. Heat a pan until a drop of water sizzles. Add half the oil and heat again. Fry veal until golden brown.
4. Add mushrooms to pan and stir gently.
5. Add wine, thyme and black pepper, cover and cook together for 10 minutes.
6. Add grapes.
7. Heat cognac almost to a boil and pour over the veal and mushrooms.
8. Ignite and serve immediately. Allow flame to burn out. Do not blow out.

280 Calories per serving

GIGANDA PASTA SHELLS, FLORENTINE

(serves 6)

10 oz. jumbo shells

1. Cook shells according to directions. Undercook, as shells will be baked. Drain, set aside.

Filling
12 oz. low-fat cottage cheese or whey cheese
2 egg whites
½ cup seasoned bread crumbs
½ tsp. nutmeg
1/8 tsp. black pepper
10-oz. package chopped frozen spinach, cooked and drained dry

1. Combine cheese, egg whites, bread crumbs, nutmeg, pepper and spinach and mix well.
2. Stuff mixture into shells.

Sauce
1 large onion, chopped
¼ cup stock or water
1 tsp. garlic powder
1 tsp. sugar
1 tsp. oregano
1 tsp. sweet basil
1 tsp. black pepper
1 cup cold water
1 1-pound can tomato puree
2 Tbsp. red wine vinegar
2 Tbsp. Parmesan cheese

1. To prepare sauce, simmer onions until golden brown, adding more water if necessary.
2. Add garlic powder, sugar, oregano, basil, pepper, cold water, tomato puree, vinegar, and cook for 30 minutes.
3. Place a few tablespoons of sauce on bottom of casserole.
4. Arrange stuffed shells carefully, just touching each other to support each other in upright position, cheese side up.
5. Spoon sauce carefully over all and bake for 20 minutes in preheated 350° oven.
6. Sprinkle with Parmesan cheese just before serving.

300 Calories for each serving of 4 shells

MANDARIN STEAK WITH VEGETABLES

(serves 6)

1 pound lean round steak
1 Tbsp. oil for stir-fry
2 cups fresh mushrooms, sliced
2 cups fresh string beans, sliced
2 cups fresh carrots, cut into thin strips
2 cups fresh broccoli, with stems cut into thin strips
2 cups fresh Chinese cabbage, shredded
4 green onions with stems, sliced
2 cups cooked brown rice (reserve for **Assemblage**)

1. Trim off all visible fat, and cut steak into ¼-inch thin strips.

2. Heat pan until a drop of water sizzles, add oil, and heat again, stir frying thin beef strips rapidly for about 3 minutes.

3. Remove meat with slotted spoon. Drain on paper towels and set aside.

4. Heat pan again reusing oil used for browning meat and stir-fry as many vegetables as will comfortably fit at one time. See that vegetables remain crisp and retain their color. Add small amount of water if necessary from time to time.

5. Remove vegetables to warm platter.

Sauce

1¼ cups cold water
3 Tbsp. cornstarch
¼ tsp. ground ginger
½ tsp. garlic powder
½ tsp. dry mustard
2 tsp. sugar
1/8 tsp. white pepper
4 Tbsp. dry sherry

1. Place water and cornstarch in tightly covered jar and shake vigorously until blended.

2. Add seasonings and wine and shake again.

3. Heat sauce to desired consistency, stirring constantly. It should be thick.

Assemblage:

1. Meanwhile, return all vegetables and meat to fry pan or wok and heat quickly until steaming hot.

2. Pour sauce over all and continue to stir-fry, tossing until thoroughly coated with sauce.

3. Serve immediately on bed of rice.

330 Calories per serving

MEATLESS LASAGNA

(serves 6)

12 oz. Lasagna noodles

Sauce

2   cups tomatoes in puree
1 large tomato, chopped
1 large onion, chopped
1 carrot, chopped or grated
1 stalk celery, chopped
½ tsp. oregano
½ tsp. garlic powder
½ tsp. basil
10 oz. mushrooms, sliced
1 cup fat-free cottage or whey cheese
2 Tbsp. seasoned bread crumbs
1 egg white
2 oz. Mozzarella, sliced into 8 slices
2 Tbsp. Parmesan cheese

1. Cook noodles according to directions.
2. Combine all sauce ingredients in a large saucepan and simmer for 30 minutes.
3. Cool and then puree in blender.
4. Add mushrooms to pureed sauce,- return to flame and cook 15 minutes at low simmer. Do not boil.
5. Combine cheese, crumbs and egg white and refrigerate for 10-15 minutes.
6. Place a small amount of sauce in bottom of large flat casserole and arrange lasagna noodles side by side, slightly overlapping to cover bottom.
7. Pour, or spoon on about ⅓ sauce.
8. Using half the cottage cheese mixture drip into 8 mounds over the noodles.
9. Cover with another layer of noodles, sauce, cheese mixture and repeat, ending with noodles and use remaining sauce to cover top.
10. Cover with the eight slices of Mozzarella cheese, and sprinkle with the Parmesan cheese.
11. Bake in preheated 350° oven for 30 minutes.
12. Remove from oven and let set for 5 minutes before serving.

290 Calories per serving.

NOODLE CHARLOTTE

(serves 8)

8 oz. package of broad noodles
1 whole egg and 1 egg white
2 cups skim milk
1 Tbsp. sugar
8 oz. fat-free cottage or whey cheese
1 8-oz. can crushed pineapple in its own
   juice
1 large apple, quartered and then sliced
   paper thin

1. Cook according to directions and
   drain.
2. Beat eggs into milk.
3. Add sugar and cheese and mix.
4. Drain pineapple and add it, along with
   the apple. Reserve the pineapple juice
   for another use.
5. Add noodles and mix all until well
   blended.

6. Pour into lightly oiled baking pan. If a
   lot of crushty top is desired, place in
   low flat pan. If a softer pudding is
   desired, use a deeper pan.

Strussel topping
1 tsp. sweet whipped butter, softened
½ cup graham crackers, crushed into
crumbs
½ tsp. cinnamon
1 tsp. sugar

7. Add strussel topping ingredients and
   press together.
8. Distribute over top of Charlotte.
9. Bake in preheated 350° oven for 45
   minutes or until set. Place under
   broiler for 3 to 5 minutes for browning
   if desired.

250 Calories per serving

PASTA PRIMAVERA

(serves 6)

12 frozen artichoke hearts cut in half
2 cooked carrots, sliced
12 small white onions, either freshly steamed
   or canned ones
½ pound cooked fresh string beans
1½ cups cooked macaroni, shells or elbows
½ tsp. tarragon
1/8 tsp. black pepper
4 oz. mozzarella cheese

1. Drain all vegetables, reserving ½ cup
   of vegetable juice.

2. Combine all vegetables with cooked
   macaroni . . . use as much of the
   vegetable juice as needed to keep
   moist.
3. Sprinkle with tarragon and pepper and
   toss lightly.
4. Arrange sliced mozzarella over top of
   vegetables.
5. Bake 20 minutes in preheated 350°
   oven. Serve immediately.

190 Calories per serving

QUICK EASY CHEAP BAKED CHICKEN

(serves 6)

1 3½-pound frying chicken
¼ tsp. garlic powder
¼ tsp. paprika
¼ tsp. black pepper
¼ tsp. sage
2 Tbsp. frozen orange concentrate

1. Remove all visible fat from chicken and then truss and tie it.
2. Pat skin dry and place chicken on a rack in baking pan.
3. Sprinkle all over with garlic powder, paprika, pepper and sage.
4. Bake in preheated 350° oven for 2 hours.
5. Baste with orange concentrate last 20 minutes for glaze and crisping. Increase temperature to 400° at this time if really crisp chicken is desired.
6. Discard fat drippings and serve immediately.

160 Calories per serving

SESAME SEASONED FISH BAKE

(serves 6)

1½ pounds flounder fillets, in 6 portions. Cod or haddock may be substituted
¼ tsp. oil
2 large cloves garlic, crushed
1 Tbsp. sweet whipped butter or margarine
2 Tbsp. lemon juice
2 Tbsp. brandy
3 Tbsp. sesame seeds
Dash of black pepper
Fresh parsley and lemon wedges for garnish

1. Drain fish dry and pat with paper towels. Allow to dry further on paper towels.
2. Arrange fish fillets on bottom of large oven casserole which has been lightly greased with the oil.
3. Combine remaining ingredients and simmer in saucepan for 5 minutes. Pour sauce over fish fillets in casserole.
4. Bake in preheated 400° oven for 12-15 minutes, or until fish is flaky and snow white.
5. Garnish with fresh parsley and lemon wedges.
6. Serve immediately from baking casserole to keep fish from breaking apart.

145 Calories per serving

SPANISH OMELET

(serves 1)

½ small onion, chopped fine
¼ green pepper, cut in thin strips
2 mushrooms, thinly sliced
¼ cup water for simmering
½ red, ripe tomato, chopped fine
2 whole eggs
1 Tbsp. skim milk
Dash of black pepper
1 tsp. butter or margarine

1. Starting with onion, simmer until tender. Add green pepper, then mushrooms and then chopped tomato.
2. Simmer together until all have blended and are tender, which should take about 5 minutes.
3. Increase heat to evaporate liquid and lightly brown vegetables.
4. Be sure that eggs are at room temperature. Whisk eggs with milk. Add black pepper.
5. Heat pan until a drop of water sizzles. Add butter and heat again. Pour in egg mixture, move egg from edges as it sets to center of pan. It will shape up as a round omelet.
6. Add the vegetable mixture as soon as the omelet sets. Fold over.
7. Cover. Turn off heat and allow to stand for 3 minutes or until remaining egg has set. Serve immediately.

230 Calories per omelet

SPEEDY SPAGHETTI SKILLET SUPPER

(serves 6)

1 pound lean ground beef

Sauce
1 6-oz. can tomato paste
1 1-pound can tomatoes in puree
1 cup cold water
1 tsp. chili powder
½ tsp. garlic powder
1 tsp. sugar
1 tsp. oregano
1 tsp. sweet basil
6 oz. spaghetti, uncooked

1. Render fat from meat in heavy pan. Drain and discard the fat.
2. Mash or crush tomatoes and combine them with all the sauce ingredients. Simmer for 30 minutes.
3. Add meat and spaghetti and cook for about 10 minutes more, stirring occasionally.
4. Allow to stand for 5 minutes before serving.

290 Calories per serving

STUFFED CABBAGE, HUNGARIAN STYLE

(serves 6)

1 large green cabbage
1 large onion, sliced in thin rings

Filling for cabbage rolls
1 cup cooked rice
½ pound lean ground veal
1 onion, finely chopped
1 Tbsp. fresh parsley
1/8 tsp. black pepper

Sauce
Juice of one lemon
2 Tbsp. honey
¼ cup raisins
2 cups canned tomatoes in puree; mash
   tomatoes first
3 cloves
1 cup cold water

1. Invert cabbages and slam down on counter to loosen core.
2. Remove core with sharp knife and place cabbage in large pot.
3. Pour several quarts of boiling water into cavity and gently press leaves apart with wooden spoon.
4. Remove leaf by leaf as they soften and set them on clean towel to drain. You will need at least 12 good leaves for stuffing.
5. Chop the remaining cabbage into small chunks and place it with onion rings in bottom of large pot.
6. Combine all ingredients for filling and toss; do not press down.
7. Divide into 12 portions and place one portion in center of each cabbage leaf. Roll, tucking in ends as best you can; they will stay together if handled gently.
8. Place each roll in pot on top of cabbage and onion rings.
9. Combine all ingredients for sauce and cook for 10 minutes.
10. Pour sauce over each roll and around sides and bottom of pot and simmer slowly for 2½ to 3 hours. Do not mix, but move gently from time to time.
11. Cool to remove any fat that may rise.
12. Serve hot.

175 Calories for 2 cabbage rolls

STUFFED CHICKEN PARTS

(serves 6)

2½ pounds of chicken parts, excepting wings, divided into 6 serving portions
6 Tbsp. seasoned bread crumbs
2 Tbsp. stock or water
1/8 tsp. paprika
Dash of garlic powder
Dash of black pepper

1. Remove all visible fat from chicken.
2. Combine crumbs with stock or water for stuffing.
3. Make a pocket in each piece of chicken by slicing as deeply as you can into thigh, leg and breast parts.
4. Stuff 1 tablespoon of stuffing into each pocket.
5. Tie with thin kite string and arrange in baking pan on rack.
6. Sprinkle with paprika and black pepper, and garlic if desired.
7. Bake in preheated 400° oven for 45 minutes, or until chicken is tender and crisp.
8. Remove from oven and cut strings.
9. Discard fat drippings and skin and serve.

195 Calories per serving

TUNA-ORZO-BROCCOLI BAKE

(serves 6)

1 cup cooked Orao (a rice-shaped macaroni product)
2 7-oz. cans tuna in water, white meat solid pack
2 cups of basic medium white sauce (see BASIC SAUCES)
12 oz. mushrooms, sliced
¼ tsp. black pepper
½ tsp. onion powder or 1 tsp. onion flakes
2 tsp. fresh parsley or ½ tsp. dried parsley
2 oz. Provolone cheese, grated
½ pound fresh or frozen broccoli, steamed and drained
½ cup seasoned bread crumbs
1 Tbsp. skim milk
1 tsp. butter or margarine
Paprika for garnish

1. Drain tuna. Flake it, do not chop.
2. Heat white sauce until desired thickness is reached and then add mushrooms, pepper, onion powder, parsley and cheese.
3. Cook 10 minutes, stirring frequently.
4. Add tuna and cook 5 minutes.
5. Arrange macaroni along bottom and up the sides of baking pan.
6. Arrange broccoli over macaroni.
7. Pour tuna-cheese sauce over all.
8. Combine crumbs, milk and butter and spread mixture over top.
9. Sprinkle with small amount of paprika and bake in preheated 350° oven for 20 minutes.

230 Calories per serving

TURKEY DIVAN

(serves 8)

2 cups basic medium white sauce (see
   BASIC SAUCES)
½ pound mushrooms, sliced
1 Tbsp. dry chives
¼ tsp. black pepper
3 cups leftover cooked turkey cut into
   ½-inch cubes
3 oz. Swiss cheese, grated
1 cup cooked brown rice
Paprika for garnish
Parsley for garnish

1. Heat sauce to desired consistency.
2. Add mushrooms, chives and black pepper and cook for 5 minutes.
3. Add turkey cubes and cook 5 miutes. Add Swiss cheese and cook five minutes more.
4. Place cooked rice along bottom of casserole.
5. Pour turkey, cheese mixture over rice.
6. Sprinkle paprika lightly on top and bake in preheated 350° oven for 30 minutes.
7. Serve immediately, garnished with parsley.

255 Calories per serving

VEAL FRANCESE

(serves 6)

1½ pounds veal cutlets
3 Tbsp. pancake flour
2 Tbsp. skim milk
1 egg white
1 Tbsp. oil
Juice of 1 lemon
½ cup dry white wine
1/8 tsp. black pepper
Parsley for garnish
Lemon slices for garnish

1. Trim off all visible fat on cutlets and cut into 6 thin slices. Pound paper-thin.
2. Combine pancake flour, milk and egg white, whisking together.
3. Dip each cutlet into batter, coating with your fingers if necessary to be sure the meat is all coated.
4. Heat pan until a drop of water sizzles; add ½ Tbsp. oil and heat again.
5. Fry cutlets on both sides to golden brown, using remaining oil as needed. Keep warm in pan.
6. Combine lemon juice, wine and black pepper to add to veal in pan.
7. Simmer covered for 5 minutes, turning cutlets to be sure all liquid is absorbed.
8. Garnish with fresh sprigs of parsley and very thinly cut lemon slices.

260 Calories per serving

VEAL MARSALA

(serves 6)

1½ pounds veal cutlets
½ cup Marsala wine
¼ tsp. garlic powder plus 1 whole clove of
   garlic, minced
2 Tbsp. fresh parsley, chopped
1/8 tsp. black pepper
½ tsp. sweet basil

1. Trim off all visible fat from veal and divide into 12 thin slices.
2. Heat wine in heavy pan and add garlic, garlic powder, parsley, pepper and basil.
3. Bring to a simmer and add cutlets.
4. Cover and simmer for 5 minutes on each side.

220 Calories per serving

VEAL MILANESE WITH PINK SAUCE

(serves 6)

1½ pounds veal cutlets cut into 12 thin slices
2 Tbsp. skim milk
2 Tbsp. whole wheat flour
1 Tbsp. oil

Sauce
½ cup red wine
¼ cup stock
8 oz. can tomato sauce
¼ tsp. garlic powder
½ tsp. basil
¼ tsp. oregano
1/8 tsp. black pepper

1. Trim off all visible fat from veal and pound paper-thin.
2. Dip veal in milk and then flour lightly, coating all sides.
3. Heat pan until a drop of water sizzles. Add oil and heat again.
4. Fry veal until golden brown on both sides. Keep warm until ready to serve.
5. Combine sauce ingredients and simmer for 20 minutes over medium heat. Serves sauce in a small serving bowl along with the veal.

255 Calories per serving

VEAL PICCATA

(serves 6)

1½ pounds veal cutlets
1 egg white, beaten
½ cup bread crumbs, seasoned
1 Tbsp. oil

Sauce
½ cup sherry
¼ cup chicken stock
Juice of 1 lemon
10 oz. mushrooms, sliced
1/8 tsp. black coarse ground pepper
½ tsp. garlic powder

Parsley for garnish
Cherry tomatoes for garnish

1. Cut veal into 12 portions and trim off all visible fat.
2. Dip cutlets in beaten egg white and coat with bread crumbs.
3. Heat pan until a drop of water sizzles. Add ½ Tbsp. oil and heat again.
4. Add veal using remaining oil as necessary, fry to golden brown on both sides. Keep warm in pan.
5. Combine sauce ingredients and simmer 10 minutes.
6. Pour over cutlets in frying pan and simmer 5 minutes longer.
7. Arrange on warmed serving platter and heap mushrooms on top of each cutlet. Garnish with cherry tomatoes and parsley.

265 Calories per serving

VEAL SCALLOPINE

(serves 6)

1½ pounds veal cutlets cut into 6 portions
2 Tbsp. whole wheat flour
1 Tbsp. oil
½ cup chicken stock
½ cup dry white wine
¼ tsp. fresh black pepper
¼ tsp. garlic powder

1. Pound veal paper-thin.
2. Dust with flour.
3. Heat pan until a drop of water sizzles. Add ½ Tbsp. oil and heat again.
4. Add veal and fry until golden brown on both sides.
5. Add remaining ingredients to frying pan and stir gently. Be sure cutlets are free of bottom of pan so sauce can be absorbed.
6. Simmer slowly for 20 minutes. Keep covered for first 10 minutes and allow steam to escape for last 10 minutes. Serve immediately.

250 Calories per serving

VEGETABLES AU GRATIN

(serves 6)

1 cup stock or water for cooking
1 medium cauliflower, in flowerettes
1 pound mushrooms, cut in half
3 medium onions, cut into eights
1 sweet fresh red pepper, cut into strips
¼ cup seasoned bread crumbs
2 tsp. softened sweet whipped butter or
   margarine
4 Tbsp. Parmesan cheese
2 oz. Mozzarella cheese

1. Starting with ½ cup water or stock simmer each vegetable until just par-cooked, reserving cooking water and adding more as needed.
2. Drain excess liquid, using only as much as needed to keep vegetables moist.
3. Combine all vegetables and toss lightly.
4. Arrange vegetables in oven casserole.
5. Mix seasoned crumbs, butter and Parmesan cheese.
6. Distribute on top of vegetables in casserole.
7. Slice Mozzarella into 6 even portions and place on top of bread crumb topping.
8. Bake 20 minutes in preheated 350° oven or until cheese melts.
9. Serve immediately.

170 Calories per serving

WINE BARBECUE CHICKEN

(serves 6)

3 pounds chicken, cut into 12 pieces

Sauce
1 medium onion, chopped fine
¼ cup stock
1 tsp. prepared mustard
1 tsp. paprika
¼ tsp. coarsely ground black pepper
¼ tsp. garlic powder
½ cup tomato sauce
½ cup tomato paste
½ cup sauterne wine

1. Remove all visible fat from chicken.
2. Heat pan over high heat.
3. Brown chicken on all sides, but do not cook.
4. Remove from pan and discard fat. Drain chicken on paper towels.
5. Simmer onion in stock until dark golden brown.
6. Add remaining ingredients to onions.
7. Stir and simmer for 15 minutes.
8. Arrange chicken on bottom of baking pan and pour hot sauce over all.
9. Bake in preheated 350° oven for 30 to 45 minutes, until chicken appears crusty and tender.
10. Serve hot after chilling to remove all fat.

185 Calories per serving

vegetables

The easiest way to prepare and serve vegetables is to steam or bake them and use herbs, spices, and a little lemon or lime juice to perk up their flavor. There really is no substitute for fresh vegetables, but when they are not available, look for frozen vegetables that have no added salt. This is impossible in the case of peas. We try to avoid using canned vegetables because of the added salt, unless it's specially packed. We do use canned tomatoes, but there is a no-salt added tomato pack available on the regular super-market shelf. Look for it.

PARSLIED ARTICHOKE HEARTS

(serves 6)

½ tsp. garlic powder
1/8 tsp. fresh ground pepper
¼ cup fresh parsley, chopped
1 tsp. lemon juice
½ cup chicken stock
1 8-oz. can artichoke hearts

1. Combine spices, juice and stock and simmer 5 minutes.
2. Add artichoke hearts and simmer until heated thoroughly.

50 Calories per serving

If frozen artichokes are used, simmer in stock until tender.

ARTICHOKE HEARTS WITH CARROTS AND ONIONS

(serves 6)

2 carrots
12 small white onions, cleaned
6 canned artichoke hearts, halved
2 tsp. fresh dill or ½ tsp. dried
1 Tbsp. lemon juice

1. Scrape and thinly slice carrots on a diagonal.
2. Cook onions and carrots in a small amount of boiling water until tender.
3. Add artichokes to carrots and onion.
4. Combine lemon juice and dill with ¼ cup vegetable liquid. Add to vegetables and simmer another 5 minutes.

50 Calories per serving

STUFFED ARTICHOKE

(serves 1)

1 medium artichoke
2 Tbsp. seasoned bread crumbs
1 tsp. melted butter or margaine
1 Tbsp. Parmesan cheese
1 tsp. parsley, chopped

1. Cut off stem. Trim off outer edges. Cut off a bit of the tips and discard. Dip tips of artichoke in lemon juice. Cook in covered pot with 2-3 inches of water for 35-40 minutes or until a leaf comes off easily. Remove and place upside down to drain.
2. Combine bread crumbs, butter, cheese and parsley.
3. Add a little skim milk if necessary to hold bread crums together.
4. Gently spread leaves apart to expose center of artichoke and remove fuzzy choke.
5. Stuff with breadcrumb mixture and bake covered in preheated 350° oven.

150 Calories per serving

This can be used as a main dish for lunch. Start with a soup and follow it with a nice salad.

asparagus

Asparagus is very low in calories — 66 per pound. Cut off base and reserve them for making asparagus soup. Steam asparagus for no more than 10 minutes. They are best slightly crisp.

Serve with fresh herbs or a bit of dried dill or tarragon. Squeeze a little fresh lemon juice or lime juice over the asparagus to perk up the taste.

When served with Hollandaise Sauce add 17 calories per teaspoon. 12 calories for 4 stalks.

BEETS WITH MANDARIN ORANGES

(serves 6)

½ pound fresh beets or 1 cup canned beets
1 cup mandarin oranges
1 tsp. lemon juice

1. Cook beets for 1 hour in boiling water in a covered pot or until tender.
2. Cool slightly before removing skin and cutting into thin slices.
3. Add oranges, lemon juice and stir.
4. Serve immediately.

30 Calories per serving

BEETS VINAIGRETTE

(serves 6)

½ pound fresh beets cut in strips juilienne style or 1 cup canned beets
2 Tbsp. orange juice
2 Tbsp. lemon juice
4 Tbsp. beet juice
2 tsp. sugar
Pinch of powdered cloves

1.   Combine cold beets with juices and spices.
2.   Marinate for 24 hours.

25 Calories per serving

To retain color of beets while cooking, leave on a bit of the stem.

broccoli

Broccoli can be eaten raw or cooked. Cut off the tough stalks and reserve for making broccoli soup. Steam the flowerettes for about 10 minutes. They taste best when slightly crunchy.

Serve with tarragon or lemon juice or both, if you like.

30 Calories per spear or for ½ cup frozen chopped broccoli

BROCCOLI SOUFFLE

(serves 8)

2 cups medium white sauce (see BASIC SAUCES)
2 tsp. dry mustard
¼ tsp. fresh ground white pepper,
1 pkg. frozen chopped broccoli (approximately 10 oz.)
4 egg whites
2 tsp. oil
Souffle dish

1.   Heat white sauce.
2.   Add mustard and pepper.
3.   Cook brocoli according to directions. Drain well.
4.   Beat egg whites with a wire whisk or electric beater until they stand up in peaks.

5.   Fold egg whites into cooled white sauce.
6.   Add sauce to broccoli gently folding broccoli and sauce together. *Do not beat.*
7.   Grease souffle dish and pour in broccoli mixture.
8.   Bake in preheated 350° oven for 30 minutes. DO NOT open oven during baking. Serve immediately.

55 Calories per serving

BRUSSEL SPROUTS WITH RED GRAPES

(serves 6)

1 qt. brussel sprouts
½ cup red grapes

1. Remove ends and any yellowed outer leaves of brussel sprouts. Wash thoroughly.
2. Steam about 10 minutes or until tender.
3. Wash grapes. Slice in half and remove seeds.
4. Place in steamer with sprouts for 2 minutes. Serve hot.

45 Calories per serving

STIR-FRIED CABBAGE

(serves 6)

1 Tbsp. oil
2 Tbsp. dry sherry
2 Tbsp. stock
1 tsp. caraway seeds
1/8 tsp. freshly ground black pepper
½ pound cabbage, shredded

1. Combine oil, sherry, stock, pepper and seeds and simmer 2 minutes.
2. Add cabbage and stir until cabbage wilts.

45 Calories per serving

CARROTS WITH PINEAPPLE

(serves 6)

3 carrots (about ½ pound)
½ cup crushed pineapple in its own juice

1. Scrape and cut carrots in thin diagonal slices.
2. Steam until tender.
3. Combine carrots and pineapple and simmer together for 5 minutes.

25 Calories per serving

HONEYED BELGIAN CARROTS

(serves 6)

¾ pound Belgian miniature carrots
1 Tbsp. honey
2 Tbsp. orange juice
1 tsp. fresh mint, chopped

1. Cook carrots in a small amount of boiling water until tender, reducing the water to about 2 Tbsp.

2. (Add honey and orange juice to carrots and simmer 5 minutes.

3. Sprinkle with chopped mint and serve hot.

35 Calories per serving

cauliflower

Cauliflower is good either raw of cooked. Use it raw in vegetable platters or marinate it in vinaigrette dressing. To cook, divide into flowerettes and steam for 10 minutes. Serve with a little chopped fresh fennel.

30 Calories per cup

CREAMED CAULIFLOWER

(serves 8)

1 large head cauliflower (about 2 pounds)
2 cups medium white sauce (see BASIC SAUCES)
2 Tbsp. Parmesan cheese

1. Trim cauliflower and divide into flowerettes. Cut stalks into small pieces.

2. Steam for 10 minutes until tender.

3. Combine sauce and cauliflower. Place in a casserole. Sprinkle with Parmesan cheese and bake in preheated 350° oven for 20 minutes.

60 Calories per serving

BREAISED CELERY AND ONIONS

(serves 6)

12 small pearled onions (about ½ pound)
½ bunch celery, cut into ½-inch slices
1 cup vegetable stock
1 tsp. butter or margarine
1/8 tsp. freshly ground black pepper

1. Simmer onions and celery in stock until tender, reducing liquid to 2 Tbsp.
2. Add butter and pepper and serve immediately.

25 Calories per serving

GREEN BEANS

(serves 6)

1 pound green beans, with ends cut off
Any herb, as dill, marjoram, parsley or
   tarragon

1. Steam beans for about 10-12 minutes until tender, but still crisp.
2. Sprinkle with any herb and serve hot.

20 Calories per serving

VARIATIONS: 1 Tbsp. sesame seeds. Add 15 Calories per serving.
   1 oz. slivered almonds. Add 30 calories per serving.

mushrooms

The mushroom is one of our most versatile vegetables — good on its own and in combination with many other foods. Low in calories — 30 per cup — it can be used raw in salads, sauteed with other vegetables, in cream and tomato sauces, marinated in vinaigrette dressing, sliced into soups and as a base for soup.

CREAMED MUSHROOMS AND ONIONS

(serves 6)

½ cup stock
½ cup onion, chopped
½ pound mushrooms, sliced
1 cup medium white sauce
2 Tbsp. parsley, chopped

1. Simmer onion in stock until tender.
2. Add mushrooms and simmer 3 minutes.
3. Add mushrooms and onions to heated white sauce. Simmer together 5 minutes.
4. Sprinkle with parsley and serve hot.

40 Calories per serving

GREEN PEAS

(serves 6)

2 pounds fresh peas, shelled
1 tsp. fresh chopped mint

1. Steam peas for 10 minutes or until tender.
2. Sprinkle with fresh mint.

50 Calories per serving

VARIATIONS: Saute 2 chopped shallots in 1 tsp. oil until tender. Add to peas and sprinkle with a dash of nutmeg. Add 7 Calories per serving.

Saute 1 cup sliced mushrooms in 1 tsp. oil. Add 8 Calories per serving

LIMA BEAN CASSEROLE

(serves 6)

1½ cups canned tomatoes
2 medium onions, thinly sliced
½ cup parsley, chopped
2 Tbsp. fresh basil or 1 Tbsp. dried
¼ tsp. black pepper
½ cup vegetable stock or juice from tomatoes
1 10-oz. package baby lima beans
2 cups shredded green letuce (Romaine or escarole are best)
2 tomatoes, sliced crosswise
1 Tbsp. Parmesan cheese

1. Simmer canned tomatoes, onions, parsley and basil in stock or juice until onions are soft.
2. Steam lima beans until tender.
3. Place small amount of sauce in baking dish.
4. Place beans, lettuce and tomatoes in layers in casserole, starting with beans.
5. Pour sauce over it and sprinkle with Parmesan cheese.
6. Bake in preheated 350° oven for 30 minutes.

100 Calories per serving

potatoes

Potatoes should be included regularly in your diet. They are an excellent source of vitamins and minerals and are easily digested. One medium potato is higher in potassium than an orange or banana and it contains Vitamin C, too. It's what you add to the potato that makes it so caloric.

BAKED STUFFED POTATO

(serves 1)

1 baking potato (about ⅓ pound)
2 Tbsp. skim milk
Dash pepper
1 tsp. parsley, chopped
Dash paprika

1. Prick potato to allow steam to escape. Bake in preheated 400° oven for one hour.
2. Slice in half lengthwise and remove insides.
3. Mix potato with milk, parsley and pepper, and stuff back into shells. Sprinkle with paprika.
4. Place on a baking sheet and bake in preheated 400° oven for 10 minutes.

100 Calories

VARIATION:
2 Tbsp. chopped spinach
Nutmeg

1. Cook spinach and drain well.
2. Add a dash of nutmeg.
3. Combine with mashed potato and stuff shells. Bake in preheated 400° oven 10 minutes.

Add 5 Calories to above.

BOILED NEW POTATOES

(serves 6)

1 pound new potatoes
¼ cup parsley, chopped

1. Scrub skins and boil whole potatoes until tender.
2. Drain and slice in ½-inch slices.
3. Toss with parsley and serve.

50 Calories per serving

SCALLOPED POTATOES

(serves 6)

1 cup low-fat cottage cheese
½ cup skim milk
1 pound potatoes, 4 medium
1/8 tsp. black pepper
1 tsp. parsley, chopped
½ tsp. onion powder

1. Combine cheese and milk in blender until creamy.

2. Peel raw potatoes and slice thinly.
3. Layer in baking pan and cover with cheese sauce.
4. Sprinkle with freshly ground black pepper and bake in preheated 350° oven for 45 minutes.

85 Calories per serving

spinach

Spinach is another one of those vegetables that can be eaten raw or cooked and is so versatile that we have used it often in our recipes. Although it is higher in sodium than most vegetables (about 60 mg. for a 4-oz. serving), it is still nothing to be concerned about unless you are on a very low salt diet.

BAKED SPINACH ROSEMARY

(serves 8)

2 10-oz. packages chopped frozen spinach
1 cup cooked brown rice
1 egg and 2 egg whites
⅓ cup evaporated skim milk
½ tsp. crushed rosemary
¼ tsp. oil

1. Cook spinach and drain well.
2. Combine rice, eggs and milk and add to spinach.

3. Grease a 1-quart baking dish and pour spinach mixture into it.
4. Bake in a preheated 350° oven for 25 minutes or until edges come free.

65 Calories per serving

sweet potatoes

Although sweet potatoes are quite caloric, you might want to budget them in occasionally, particularly at Thanksgiving time. One pound of sweet potatoes has 394 calories as compared to plain potatoes which have 280 calories per pound. Baking them in their skins for one hour in a hot oven is the most economical way calorically.

SWEET POTATOES WITH COGNAC

(serves 6)

2 cups mashed sweet potatoes
2 Tbsp. cognac
1/8 tsp. cinnamon

Combine cognac and cinnamon with mashed sweet potatoes.

100 Calories per serving

VARIATION: Place potatoes on pineapple slices canned in its own juice. Bake 20 minutes. Add 35 Calories for each pineapple slice.

SWEET POTATOES

(serves 6)

1½ cups cooked sweet potatoes
1 cup crushed pineapple in its own juice

1. Mash potatoes and combine with crushed pineapple.

2. Place in a casserole and bake in preheated 350° oven for 30 minutes.

90 Calories per serving

CANDIED SWEET POTATOES

(serves 6)

2 cups cooked sweet potatoes
½ cup orange juice
1 Tbsp. honey
1/8 tsp. cinnamon

1. Slice in ¼-inch slices and place in baking dish.

2. Combine orange juice, honey and cinnamon.
3. Pour over potatoes and bake in preheated 350° oven for 30 minutes, basting frequently.

105 Calories per serving

ZUCCHINI-TOMATO CHEESE CASSEROLE

(serves 6)

1 cup tomato sauce
1 large onion, sliced in rings
2 pounds zucchini, thinly sliced
½ pound mushrooms, sliced
1 pound tomtoes, thinly sliced
1 tsp. fresh basil, chopped
1 tsp. oregano
2 oz. Tilsit cheese
¼ cup seasoned breadcrumbs
1 Tbsp. Parmesan cheese

1. Place a little sauce in the bottom of a casserole.
2. Layer the vegetables, starting with the onions, and then the zucchini, mushrooms and tomatoes.
3. Sprinkle with oregano and basil. Pour remaining sauce over the vegetables.
4. Cut cheese into small pieces and distribute across top.
5. Sprinkle with breadcrumbs and Parmesan cheese.
6. Cover casserole. Bake in preheated 350° oven for 30 minutes.

120 Calories per serving

baked goods

The baked goods in this section are a specially selected group of pies, cakes, cookies, breads and muffins that have been carefully tested for texture and taste. The caloric values vary in each, some being higher than others. Give your attention to the portions involved. No harm in a delicious piece of cheesecake, or apple pie occasionally, provided that you are aware of the calories and have taken them into consideration.

APPLE CHEESEPIE

(serves 8)

8 oz. fat-free whey cheese or low-fat cottage cheese
2 Tbsp. sugar
1 egg
½ cup plain low-fat yogurt
1 tsp. lemon juice
½ tsp. cinnamon
1 tsp. vanilla extract
2 large apples, peeled and thinly sliced
1 cup grapenuts (cereal)
1 tsp. sugar
¼ tsp cinnamon

1. Combine cheese, sugar, egg and yogurt and mix well.
2. Sprinkle lemon juice, cinnamon and vanilla extract over sliced apples.
3. Spread grapenuts evenly over bottom of pan.
4. Carefully arrange apple mixture over grapenuts so you do not disturb bottom.
5. Pour cheese mixture over all. Sprinkle with cinnamon and sugar mixture.
6. Bake in preheated 350° oven for 30 minutes or until inserted knife comes out clean.

125 Calories per serving

APPLE PIE-ZWIEBACK CRUST

(serves 8)

4 pieces Zwieback, crushed into crumbs
1 Tbsp. oil or butter
2 Tbsp. skim milk
6 sweet red apples
1 Tbsp. lemon juice
1 tsp. cinnamon
Pinch nutmeg
1 tsp. sugar
3 more pieces of Zwieback, crushed
½ tsp. sugar

1. Add butter and milk to first mixture of Zwieack crumbs and press into pie pan.

2. Peel, core and slice apples into 16ths.
3. Toss apples with flavoring and arrange over Zwieback crust.
4. Combine the other Zwieback crumbs with the sugar and sprinkle over apple mixture.
5. Bake in preheated 375° oven for 45 minutes or until apples are tender.
6. Cool on rack. Allow to "set" for 10 minutes.
7. Serve warm.

110 Calories per serving

APPLE RAISIN OATMEAL COOKIES

(30 cookies)

¼ cup oil
⅓ cup sugar
1 egg
1 red apple
2 Tbsp. water
¼ cup raisins
1 cup sifted enriched flour
¼ tsp. baking powder
¼ cup oatmeal
½ tsp. cinnamon
2 Tbsp. water
¼ tsp. oil

1. Combine oil, sugar, egg and cream together.
2. Peel, core and chop apple.

3. Simmer chopped apple in water for 3-5 minutes until tender.
4. Add raisins to hot mixture.
5. Mix remaining dry ingredients together.
6. Add sugar mixture to dry ingredients using as much of the water as needed to form proper consistency for drop-ping dough by teaspoon onto oiled cookie sheet.
7. Bake in preheated 350° oven for 12 to 15 minutes.
8. Remove from cookie sheet immediate-ly for softer cookie.
9. Allow to cool on cookie sheet if crisper cookie is desired.

50 Calories each cookie

APPLE STRUDEL

(serves 6)

2 sheets of Phyllo leaves

Filling
½ pound of ripe apples, peeled and sliced
2 Tbsp. raisins
½ tsp. cinnamon
1 tsp. lemon juice
1 Tbsp. skim milk

Prepare leaves according to directions on box but elminiate the use of oil.
1. Combine all filling ingredients except milk. Spread mixture on leaves and about 2 inches from edge.
2. Roll up jelly-roll fashion.
3. Place on oiled baking sheet and brush top with skim milk.
4. Bake in preheated 375° oven for 40 minutes or until golden brown and flaky.
5. Serve warm.

55 Calories per serving

BANANA BREAD

(16 slices)

1¼ cup butter or margarine
¼ cup sugar
1 egg, lightly beaten
3 medium ripe bananas, mashed(1 pound)
1½ cups enriched flour
1 tsp. baking soda
¾ cup skim milk
¼ tsp. oil

1. Cream butter and sugar.
2. Add beaten egg, mashed bananas and blend.
3. Sift flour and baking soda and stir into banana mixture.
4. Add milk and mix.
5. Pour into oiled loaf pan. Bake in preheated 350° oven for 1 hour. Test for doneness with tester or knife. Insert in center and when it comes out clean, cake is done.
6. Cool on rack.

100 Calories each slice

BISQUIT DOUGH FOR PIE CRUST

(serves 8)

¾ cup flour, sifted
1½ Tbsp. instant dry no-fat skim milk
1½ tsp. baking powder
2 Tbsp. oil
¼ cup cold water
Flour for dusting board

1. Combine flour, dry milk and baking powder.
2. Using a fork, blend in oil.
3. Sprinkle with as much water as needed to form into a ball of dough.
4. Dust board with flour.
5. Press or roll into shape for pie crust. Place in pan and prick crust with a fork to prevent bubbles.
6. Bake in preheated 350° oven for 10 minutes.
   Cool on rack before filling.

575 Calories for whole crust

BISQUIT FOR BREAKFAST

(serves 6)

½ cup flour, sifted
¾ tsp. baking powder
1 Tbsp. oil
¼ cup skim milk

1. Combine all ingredients and mix together until well blended.
2. Knead on floured board.
3. Roll or press into shape for bisquits.
4. Place on cookie tin or sheet, slightly oiled, and bake in preheated 350° oven for 15 minutes or until golden brown.

60 Calories each

VARIATION:
For Danish Cinnamon Roll
1 Tbsp. white raisins
1 tsp. sugar, light brown
½ tsp. cinnamon
2 Tbsp. skim milk

1. Roll out bisquit dough.
2. Combine raisins, sugar and cinnamon and distribute over entire surface of dough.
3. Roll up jelly-roll style and brush top with skim milk.
4. Bake in preheated 350° oven for 25 minutes.

50 additional Calories for entire filling

BLUEBERRY CRISP

(serves 6)

3 cups fresh blueberries, washed
1 tsp. sugar
1 Tbsp. lemon juice
½ cup whole wheat flour
½ cup rolled quick oats
2 Tbsp. sugar, light brown
1 Tbsp. butter or margarine

1. Toss blueberries with sugar and lemon juice. Do not mash.
2. Place in bottom of baking pan.
3. Combine flour, oats and sugar.
4. Cut in butter and mix with fork to create crumbs.
5. Sprinkle evenly over blueberries and bake in preheated 375° oven for 30 minutes. Place under broiler for 3 minutes if browner top is desired.
6. Allow to "set" for 10 minutes before serving. Serve hot.

105 Calories per serving

CEREAL CRUMB CRUST

(Makes 1 9" pie shell)

½ cup grapenuts
½ cup bran
1 Tbsp. oil
1 Tbsp. skim milk
¼ tsp. cinnamon

1. Mix grapenuts and bran.
2. Crush the cereal into crumbs.
3. Add oil, milk and cinnamon and mix.
4. Press into pie plate.
5. Bake in preheated 350° oven for 10 minutes. Cool on rack.

305 Calories for the crust

CRUNCHY APPLE GRAHAM

(serves 8)

½ cup unsweetened orange juice
1 tsp. lemon juice
1 tsp. cinnamon
6 medium apples, cored, unpeeled and sliced very thin
1 cup crushed graham crackers
¼ tsp. cinnamon

1. Combine orange juice, lemon juice and cinnamon.
2. Arrange apples in a baking pan and pour jucie over them.
3. Sprinkle crushed graham cracker crumbs over apples.
4. Bake in preheated 400° oven for 25 minutes or until apples are tender, not mushy.
Place under broiler for 3-4 minutes for browning.

100 Calories per serving

FRENCH FRUIT FLAN

(serves 10)

¾ cup unsifted flour
2 Tbsp. instant dry low-fat skim milk
1½ tsp. baking powder
1 Tbsp. unsalted butter
½ cup cold water
4 medium sized apples, ripe pears or
    peaches, or a combination of them
½ tsp. cinnamon
¼ cup sugar
8 oz. plain low-fat yogurt
1 egg white
1 tsp. vanilla extract

1. Mix flour, dry milk and baking powder.
2. Cut butter into dry ingredients, using a fork or pastry blender. Add only as much of the ½ cup of cold water as you need to make a dough that can be pressed down into pie of flan pan.
3. Press dough along bottom and up sides of flan pan. IF using pie pan, press up sides at least ¾ inch. Prick crust with fork.
4. Bake in preheated 350° oven for 15 minutes.
5. Arrange fruit attractively in continuing circles around bottom of pan directly on crust.
6. Combine cinnamon, sugar, yogurt, egg white and vanilla extract and mix briskly together.
7. Pour yogurt mixture over fruit in flan pan and bake in preheated 350° oven for 45 minutes.
8. Remove from oven and allow to "set" for 20 minutes. Serve warm.

105 Calories per serving

GRAHAM-APPLE CRISP

(serves 6)

3 medium sweet apples
½ tsp. cinnamon
1 Tbsp. lemon juice

Topping
4 graham crackers, crushed
2 Tbsp. flour
1 Tbsp. butter or margarine, softened
¼ cup cold water

1. Cut apples into thin wedges. Do not peel. Remove core.
2. Sprinkle with cinnamon and lemon juice.
3. Combine crushed crackers, flour and softened butter.
4. Arrange apples in glass baking pan.
5. Pour water into pan over and under apples.
6. Sprinkle topping mixture over apples.
7. Bake in preheated 350° oven for 25 minutes or until apples are soft and topping is browned. This can be placed under the broiler for 3 minutes to crisp.

85 Calories per serving

IRISH SODA BREAD

(serves 12)

2 cups sifted flour
1 Tbsp. sugar
1 tsp. baking soda
1 tsp. baking powder
1 Tbsp. butter or oil
1 cup buttermilk, low-fat skimmed
1 Tbsp. caraway seeds
¼ cup raisins
1 egg, whisked
1 Tbsp. skim milk

1. Assemble all ingredients in large bowl and mix. The dough will be heavy.
2. Place in well oiled round baking pan and brush top with skim milk.
3. Bake in preheated 350° oven 50 to 60 minutes.

100 Calories each slice

MERINGUE SHELLS

(makes 6)

3 egg whites at room temperature
1 tsp. vanilla extract
¼ cup sugar
¼ tsp. cream of tartar
½ tsp. oil

1. Combine egg whites with vanilla and beat until frothy.
2. Add sugar, cream of tartar and beat until stiff peaks are formed.
3. Oil large cookie sheet.
4. Shape meringue into shells with your fingers or a spoon.
5. Bake slowly in preheated 240° oven for 1 hour. If crisper shells are desired, turn off oven and allow meringue to remain in oven up to 1 hour longer.
6. Cool and fill with dessert fruits. If you eliminate the sugar, they can be used as shells for salads, vegetables or any hot foods.

45 Calories each shell

OATMEAL WHEAT MUFFINS

(Makes 12 muffins)

1 cup bran cereal
1 cup skim milk
1 egg
¼ cup honey
2 Tbsp. oil
¼ cup oatmeal
1 cup enriched flour
2 tsp. baking powder
¼ tsp. baking soda

1. Combine all ingredients and mix well. Batter will be heavy.
2. Drop into oil, coated muffin tin, filling each about ⅓ full.
3. Bake in preheated 400° oven for 20-25 minutes.

135 Calories each muffin

PERFECT POPOVERS

(Makes 12 popovers)

1 egg
1 cup skim milk
1 cup sifted enriched flour
1 tsp. oil for greasing cups

1. Combine all ingredients and beat with electric mixer 1 minute.
2. Grease coated cup cake tin.
3. Divide batter by spoonfulls into 12 portions.
4. Bake in preheated 400° oven for 10 minutes.
5. Reduce heat to 350° and bake 15 minutes longer or until golden brown.
6. Remove pan from oven and prick each popover to allow steam to escape. Then place a wet towel on a wooden surface, place pan on top, and allow popovers to cool.
7. Remove from pan. Serve immediately.

50 Calories for each popover

PINEAPPLE CHEESE PIE

(serves 8)

One pie crust from this section
1 12-oz. can unsweetened pineapple juice
1 envelope plain gelatin (1 Tbsp.)
1 Tbsp. sugar
1 8-oz. container low-fat cottage cheese

1. Heat pineapple juice and dissolve gelatin in it, stirring constantly.
2. Add sugar and continue cooking.
3. Stir until thickened and then cool slightly.
4. Add cheese and beat with electric mixer until smooth.
5. Pour into baked pie shell and chill. Refrigerate until set.

410 Calories for the pie filling

PUMPKIN BREAD

(16 slices)

2 cups sifted flour
½ cup sugar
1 tsp. baking powder
½ tsp. baking soda
2 eggs
½ tsp. cinnamon
½ tsp. nutmeg
¼ tsp. crushed cloves
¼ tsp. crushed ginger
16-oz. can pumpkin
¼ cup oil
½ cup cold water

1. Combine all ingredients and mix for 3 minutes at low speed.
2. When well blended, increase beating speed and blend for 3 minutes more.
3. Pour into oiled, large loaf pan and bake in preheated 350° oven for 1 hour. Test by inserting knife. When knife comes out clean, cake is done. May require an additional 15 minutes.
4. Cool on rack. Remove from pan after 15 minutes.

170 Calories per slice

SQUASH BREAD (YELLOW or GREEN ZUCCHINI or CARROT BREAD

(Makes 16 slices)

1½ cups unsifted flour
1 tsp. baking powder
2 tsp. baking soda
2 tsp. cinnamon
2 eggs
½ cup sugar
¼ cup oil
½ cup skim milk
2 tsp. vanilla extract
1½ cups shredded squash, lightly packed
  (do not be tempted to add more)
Carrots may be substituted

1. Mix flour, baking powder, soda and cinnamon.
2. Beat eggs. Add sugar and cream together.
3. Add oil, water and milk and mix.
4. Add vanilla extract and mix.
5. Add squash and mix until all ingredients are well blended.
6. Pour into oiled pan 9 × 5 × 3″ and bake in preheated 350° oven for 45 to 50 minutes. Test for doneness by inserting knife into center. When knife comes out clean, cake is done.
7. Cool on rack. Remove from pan after 15 minutes.

110 Calories per slice

WHEY CHEESE CAKE

(serves 10)

1½ pounds whey cheese, softened
2 Tbsp. sugar
1 tsp. vanilla extract
2 tsp. lemon juice
2 eggs
8 oz. lemon yogurt

Crust
½ cup graham cracker crumbs
1 Tbsp. skim milk to moisten crumbs
½ tsp. cinnamon

1. Mix cheese with sugar, vanilla extract, lemon juice and eggs.
2. Beat with an electric beater for 3 minutes until smooth.
3. Add half of lemon yogurt.
4. Combine graham cracker crumbs, skim milk and cinnamon and press into bottom of 8″ spring form pan.
5. Bake in preheated 350° oven for 5 minutes.
6. Cool and then pour cheese mixture into pan.
7. Bake in preheated 400° oven for 10 minutes.
8. Reduce to 250° and bake for 15 minutes longer.
9. Cool on rack and then place in refrigerator for 2 hours. Smooth remaining half of lemon yogurt evenly over top.

140 Calories per serving

desserts

There is no question that fruit, fresh or stewed, is your best bet for dessert. But somehow we couldn't let it go at that. The gauntlet had been cast down and we were challenged.

We have come up with Strudel, Crunchies, Tarts, Flans, Mousse, Crisps, Compotes, Puddings and Pies. We have Delights, Supremes, Parfaits, Medleys, Smoothies, Toppings, Whips and Slushes . . . we even have Ruffles. They are all carefully constructed, analyzed, nutritionally sound, and delicious. We may yearn for an old-fashioned three-scooper banana split with real whipped cream, but forsaking that, these desserts are real treats that treat your body well too.

AMBROSIA

(serves 10)

2 cups unsweetened pineapple juice
2 Tbsp. lemon juice
2 Tbsp. unflavored gelatin (2 packets)
1 cup mandarin oranges
1 cup peaches
½ cup grapes, pitted and halved
2 tsp. flaked coconut for topping

1. Heat the pineapple and lemon juice.
2. Add gelatin and dissolve by stirring briskly and constantly, especially along the sides and bottom.
3. Cool in refrigerator until syrupy.
4. Add fruit to thickening gelatin mixture and mix.
5. Pour into sherbet galsses and top with flaked coconut.
6. Chill. Refrigerate for 2 hours or longer.

65 Calories per serving

AMORETTA CANTALOUPE POINTS

(serves 6)

1 large ripe cantaloupe
2 cups of assorted fresh fruit
2 Tbsp. or Amoretta, Orange Brandy or
   Banana Liqueur

1. Cut thin slice form bottom of melon so that it will balance on flat surface.
2. Insert sharp knife into center at an angle of about 45°. Remove knife and insert at opposite angle, also 45°. This will create points all round as you cut in half, continuing same zig-zag.
3. Remove seeds from cavity and cut each half into thirds.
4. Fill cavity with assorted fruit in season: oranges, peaches, cherries, banana, pear, etc.
5. Drizzle liqueur over melon sections, chill and serve.

85 Calories per serving

APPLE BREAD PUDDING

(serves 8)

3 cups white bread cubes
2 cups skim milk
2 egg whites, slightly beaten
1 tsp. vanilla extract
½ tsp. cinnamon
¼ tsp. nutmeg
2 tsp. sugar
1 tsp. lemon juice
1 tsp. oil
2 medium apples, unpeeled and quartered, then sliced paper-thin

1. Place bread cubes in large mixing bowl.
2. Pour milk into another bowl, add egg whites and flavorings, and beat together with electric mixer or egg beater.
3. Lightly oil baking pan and add apple slices.
4. Pour egg and milk mixture over bread cubes and toss. Distribute over apples. Do not mash down.
5. Set pan in a larger pan of hot water and bake in preheated 350° oven for 40 minutes.

110 Calories per serving

APPLESAUCE — PINK AND TART

(serves 8)

6 medium red apples, unpeeled and sliced in ½" pieces
½ cup water
2 Tbsp. lemon juice
½ tsp. cinnamon

1. Combine apples, water, lemon and cinnamon and cook 10 minutes until tender.
2. Cool enough to place in blender and then puree.
   Serve warm or chilled.

75 Calories per serving

BANANA MOUSSE

(serves 10)

6 ripe bananas, peeled and sliced (about 2 pounds)
2 Tbsp. sugar
½ tsp. vanilla extract
1 cup evaporated skim milk
1 Tbsp. chocolate sprinkles

1. Mash bananas with fork until smooth.
2. Add sugar and vanilla extract. Set aside.
3. Chill evaporated milk and a bowl in freezer for 2 hours before using.
4. Pour milk into chilled bowl and whip it at very high speed until it forms peaks.
5. Fold in banana mixture and blend gently together.
6. Serve immediately with sprinkles for garnish.

90 Calories per serving

COMPOTE OF STEWED FRUIT

(serves 6)

Note: Choice of any 6 fruits will serve 6 people. This may be prepared in large quantities and stored for future use.

6 ripe apples, or
   peaches, or
   pears, or
   plums, or any combination of fresh fruits in season to total 6
½ cup water
2 tsp. lemon juice
½ tsp. cinnamon

1. Cut, core, do not peel fruit.
2. Slice into 16ths.
3. Combine apples with water, lemon juice and cinnamon.
4. Simmer 5 minutes, leaving fruit firm.

75 Calories per serving

CREAMY RICE PUDDING

(serves 10)

2 cups cooked white rice
2 Tbsp. sugar
3 cups scalded skim milk
1 tsp. vanilla
1 egg, beaten
¼ cup raisins
¼ tsp. cinnamon
1 tsp. butter

1. Combine all ingredients, except butter.
2. Place in buttered baking pan.
3. Place pan in shallow pan of hot water and bake in preheated 350° oven for 1½ hours. When knife comes out clean, pudding is done.

110 Calories per serving

FRESH FRUIT COMPOTE

(serves 6)

1 large orange
1 large pear
1 medium banana
4 pitted dried prunes
½ cup orange juice
1/8 tsp. nutmeg
Dash cinnamon

1. Peel, core and cut all fruit into ½-inch pieces.
2. Place fruit in a large bowl.
3. Add orange juice and nutmeg. Mix.
4. Let stand 15 minutes in refrigerator.
5. Divide fruit into 6 dessert dishes and sprinkle with a dash of cinnamon.

80 Calories per serving

FRUIT PARFAIT SUPREME

(serves 8)

8 oz. plain low-fat yogurt
1 Tbsp. sugar
½ tsp. vanilla extract
1 ripe pear, chopped
1 large orange, peeled and chopped
Flesh of 1 ripe cantaloupe
8 strawberries or fresh fruit in season for garnish

1. Mix yogurt and sugar and allow to stand in refrigerator 15 minutes.
2. Add vanilla extract.
3. Place all fruit except garnish in a large bowl and pour yogurt over all.
4. Allow to marinate several hours.
5. Serve in dessert glasses topped with fresh strawberry.

75 Calories per serving

ORANGE DELIGHT

(serves 1)

1 large orange
1 Tbsp. grated coconut
Dash nutmeg

1. Sprinkle coconut over orange slices.
2. Sprinkle nutmeg and then allow to stand 10 minutes before serving.

100 Calories per serving

ORANGE-PINEAPPLE RUM MEDLEY

(serves 8 to 10)

1 large orange
1 large ripe pineapple
2 Tbsp. dark rum

1. Place slice of orange on each slice of pineapple.
2. Distribute rum over all.
3. Allow to marinate 2 hours and then serve at room temperature.

75 Calories per serving

ORANGE SMOOTHIE

(serves 6)

6 oz. frozen orange juice concentrate
1 cup skim milk
1 cup water
¼ cup sugar
½ tsp. vanilla extract
24 ice cubes

1. Combine all ingredients including ice in blender.
2. Start on chop until ice is crushed and puree for 30 seconds.
3. Serve immediately in tall chilled glasses.

95 Calories for each 8 oz. glass

ORANGE YOGURT TOPPING
FOR FRUIT

(serves 8)

1 cup low-fat plain yogurt
3 Tbsp. frozen orange juice concentrate
1 Tbsp. powdered sugar

1. Combine yogurt, orange concentrate and sugar.
2. Mix well and chill.
3. Serve by the tablespoon over any fresh fruit.

30 Calories per serving

PEACH WHIP

(serves 6)

2 egg whites
2 cups of pureed peaches, either canned and
unsweetened or fresh stewed
1 Tbsp. honey
6 thin orange slices for garnish

1. Beat egg whites until stiff peaks will hold.
2. Fold in peach and honey mixture.
3. Pour into dessert glasses and chill.
4. Garnish with orange slice twist.

80 Calories per serving

PINEAPPLE COOLER OR
PINEAPPLE SLUSH

(serves 16)

46 oz. can unsweetened pineapple juice
2 tbsp. lemon juice
6 oz. can frozen orange juice concentrate
10 oz. bottle club soda

1. Mix together and chill thoroughly.
2. Pour into tall glasses each with 4 ice cubes. May be placed in blender with ice to make PINEAPPLE SLUSH. Serve with sprig of mint.

70 Calories each 4 oz. glass

PINEAPPLE de MENTHE

(serves 8)

1 ripe pineapple
¼ cup cold water
1 Tbsp. honey
1 Tbsp. Creme de Menthe
8 mint leaves for garnish

1. Peel, slice and quarter pineapple.
2. Simmer pineapple in water, honey and Creme de Menthe for 10 minutes.
3. Serve warm or chilled, garnished with mint leaf.

60 Calories per serving

PINEAPPLE ICE MILK

(serves 8)

1 6-oz. can concentrated frozen pineapple juice
2 cups low-fat buttermilk
1 8-oz. can crushed pineapple packed in its own juice
Ripe cherry or strawberry for garnish

1. Combine juice and buttermilk in a large bowl and beat with electric mixer.
2. Place in freezer until almost firm.
3. Beat until frothy and then add pineapple chunks with juice.
4. Pour into ice cube trays to freeze.
5. Serve in sherbet glasses with cherry or strawberry garnish.

95 Calories per serving

PINEAPPLE MOUSSE

(serves 6)

1½ cups unsweetened pineapple juice
1 Tbsp. gelatin, unflavored (1 packet)
1 Tbsp. lemon juice
1 cup skim evaporated milk
1 Tbsp. powdered sugar

1. Heat pineapple juice and add gelatin, stirring constantly until all granules have been dissolved. Scrape sides and bottom of pan.
2. Add lemon juice and refrigerate or place in freezer until mixture becomes syrupy.
3. Chill evaporated milk and a bowl in freezer for 1 hour.
4. Place milk in chilled bowl and beat on high speed with electric mixer until peaks form. Then add sugar.
5. Add to gelatin mixture as soon as milk forms peaks.
   Pour into dessert dishes. Refrigerate for several hours before serving.

90 Calories per serving

PLUM RUFFLES

(serves 6)

12 ripe Italian plums
6 oz. low-fat cottage or whey cheese
¼ cup walnuts, chopped
1 tsp. sugar

1. Steam plums for 2 minutes.
2. Drain and cool.
3. Combine cottage cheese with nuts and sugar.
4. Arrange plum halves on serving platter.
5. Divide cheese mixture into 6 portions and place an even portion on each of 6 halves. Cover with second half.
6. Press down slightly, just enough for cheese to "ruffle" out of sides.
7. Chill.

110 Calories per serving

ORANGE SPRITZER

(serves 4)

2 cups orange juice
2 cups salt-free seltzer
1 lime, cut in quarters

1. Combine juice and seltzer.
2. Squeeze lime into drink.

55 Calories per glass

ICED COFFEE MALTED

(serves 4)

4 tsp. instant coffee
1 cup water
1 cup skim milk
8 ice cubes
¼ tsp. vanilla

1. Dissolve coffee in water.
2. Place all ingredients in a blender and whip until ice cubes are completey dissolved. Serve in tall glasses.

22 Calories per glass

STRAWBERRY CREAM

(serves 10)

4 cups fresh strawberries
¼ cup sugar
2 cups plain low-fat yogurt
Whole strawberry for garnish

1. Mash strawberries with sugar.
2. Add yogurt, mix well and pour into freezer tray.
3. Freeze until firm.
4. Remove to bowl and beat with electric mixer until fluffy and smooth.
5. Divide into sherbet glasses. Freeze again if not serving immediately.
6. Garnish with whole strawberry.

65 Calories per serving

appendix

In December, 1977, after many years of listening to expert testimony from the medical and nutritional communities about the relationship between diet and health, the Select Committee on Nutrition and Human Needs of the United States Senate, chaired by Senator George McGovern, issued "Dietary Goals for the United States."

In issuing these guidelines for the American people, the government hoped to reduce the incidence of some diseases such as cardiovascular, cancer, diabetes and other that might be related to diet.

Since obesity is such a problem in the United States, the first recommendation was to keep the number of calories you consume and the number of calories you expend at a level that would keep your weight within a normal range.

The nutritional guidelines recommended by the Senate Select Committee are as follows:

Percent of Daily Intake

Carbohydrate (Starches and Sugars)   58%
No more than "10% of the 58% should be from refined sugars (cane and beet sugar) and processed sugars (honey, syrups, molasses and corn sugar.) The other 48% should be from complex carbohydrates (starches) and naturally occurring sugars."

Protein   12%
Fat   30%
The fats are equally divided among the saturated, monosaturated and polyunsaturated, giving each 10%.

Cholesterol   300 mg.
Salt   5 gms. (1 tsp.)

The guidelines that we have used in the Hamptons Health Spa Diet vary somewhat from that of the Senate Select Committee. The fat intake in our diet is limited to no more than 20%. Research has shown that in those countries, particularly the Orient, where the fat intake is less than 20%, the incidence of heart disease is much lower than in the United States. The McGovern Commission report also indicated that at some future date there might be a recommendations to reduce the fat intake below 30%. The National Academy of Sciences issued a report in June 1982 strongly advising a reduction in the consumption of fat to reduce the incidence of cancer. In addition to the possible health benefits of a reduced fat intake, it is easier to maintain a normal weight when less fat is consumed because fat contains more than twice as many calories as carbohydrate or protein.

In increasing the carbohydrate intake over the government guidlines to about 65%, we have taken great care to include whole grains, fruits and vegetables. Sugar consumption is kept to a bare minimum, well under the 10% recommendation.

Protein averages one gram per kilo (2.2 lbs.) of body weight. On a reduction diet, this is more tha 12%, but this amount of protein is necessary for maintaining good health. As caloric intake is increased, more carbohydrate foods are added.

The sodium content of our diet is under 2000 mg. of sodium. We do not add salt as such, but it is found in some of the canned product we use occasionally, as well as in bread. Of course sodium is present naturally in most foods. Animal foods contain more sodium than vegetables. The cholesterol content averages under 300 mg.

We feel that dieting with our guidelines in mind will help insure a healthier, slimmer you.

weights and measures

3 tsp	=	1 Tbsp.
4 Tbsp.	=	¼ cup
5 Tbsp. plus 1 tsp.	=	⅓ cup
8 Tbsp.	=	½ cup
16 Tbsp.	=	1 cup
1 small pinch	=	1/16 tsp.
1 large pinch	=	1/8 tsp.

Butter and margarine, not whipped

1 Tbsp.	=	½ oz.
1 stick = ½ cup = 4 oz.	=	¼ lb.
2 sticks = 1 cup = 8 oz.	=	½ lb.
2 cups	=	1 lb.
½ cup butter	=	⅓ cup vegetable oil

Cooked boned chicken

2 lbs.	=	3 cups

Egg whites

2 egg whites plus 1 Tbsp. liquid	=	1 whole egg

Flour

4 cups	=	1 lb.

Lemons

1 medium	=	2-3 Tbsp. juice
2-3 lemons	=	½ cup

Pasta

1 oz. dry	=	½ cup cooked
8 oz. dry	=	4 cups cooked

Potatoes

3 medium	=	1 lb.

Split peas and beans

2 cups uncooked	=	5 cups cooked (approximate)

Rice

1 cup uncooked	=	2½ cups cooked

Sugar, granulated

2 cups (approximate)	=	1 lb.

spice chart

	Appetizers	Soups	Fish	Meat	Poultry	Vegetable	Dessert	Salads	Sauce
Allspice	x	x	x	x	x	x	x	x	x
Basil	x	x	x	x	x	x		x	x
Bay Leaves		x	x	x	x				x
Caraway Seed		x	x			x			
Celery Seed		x	x					x	
Chives	x	x	x	x		x			x
Cinnamon							x		x
Cloves							x		
Coriander	x	x	x	x	x	x			
Cumin	x	x	x	x	x	x			
Curry	x	x	x	x	x	x			
Fennel		x	x	x					
Garlic	x	x	x	x	x	x	x	x	x
Ginger							x		
Marjoram		x	x	x	x	x	x	x	x
Mint	x			x		x	x	x	x
Mustard	x		x	x		x	x	x	x
Nutmeg							x		
Onion	x	x	x	x	x	x		x	x
Oregano	x	x	x	x	x	x		x	x

	Appetizers	Soups	Fish	Meat	Poultry	Vegetable	Dessert	Salads	Sauce
Paprika	×	×	×	×	×	×		×	×
Parsley	×	×	×	×	×	×		×	×
Pepper: Black	×	×	×	×	×	×		×	×
Red		×		×					
White	×	×	×	×	×	×		×	×
Poppy	×			×			×		
Rosemary		×		×	×	×			
Saffron					×	×			
Sage	×	×	×	×	×	×			
Savory		×	×	×		×			
Sesame			×				×		
Tarragon	×	×	×		×	×		×	×
Thyme	×	×	×	×	×				
Tumeric					×				
Vanilla							×		
Other extracts							×		
Watercress	×	×	×	×		×		×	×

calorie and nutrition chart

Food	Calories	Protein	Fat	Carbohydrate	Sodium	Cholesterol
Apple, 1 med. fresh	80	Trace	1	20	0	0
Apricot, 3 med. fresh	55	1	Trace	14	0	0
Apricot, dried raw, 1 cup	340	7	1	86	0	0
Artichoke, fresh cooked, 1 med.	53	3.5	0	12	0	0
Asparagus, fresh cooked, 4 med.	12	1	Trace	2.2	0	0
Avocado, fresh, 1 med. (10 oz.)	378	4.8	37	14	0	0
Baking Powder, 1 tsp.	6	0	0	1	276	0
Baking Soda, 1 tsp.		0	0	0	1000	0
Banana, 1 med.	101	1.3	0	26	0	0
Barley, raw, 1 cup	700	16	2	158	7	0
Bass, striped whole fish, 1 lb.	205	36.9	5.3	0	275	2
Beans, Kidney, cooked, drained, 1 cup	230	15	.8	40	15	0
Beans, Baby Lima, cooked, drained, 1 cup	210	15	1	42	15	0
Bean Sprouts, fresh, ½ cup	16	2	0	4	3	0
Beef, lean, no bone, 11% fat, uncooked, 4 oz.	227	24	14	0	75	90
Beef, lean, no bone, 18% fat, 4 oz.	292	21	22	0	75	90
Beets, canned, ½ cup	29	1.1	Trace	6.7	195	0
Blueberries, fresh, ½ cup	45	.5	.4	11	0	0
Bluefish, raw, fillet, 4 oz.	135	23	1.9	0	84	53

Bread:					
Bagel, 1 large	165	6	1	26	240	0
French, 1" thick	83	2.7	Trace	17	117	0
Pita, 1 small	80	2.7	0	17	160	0
Whole Wheat,					
very thin bread slice	40	1.3	.4	7	101	0
Bread Crumbs, un-					
seasoned, 1 tbsp.	22	.75	Trace	4	35	0
Bread Crumbs, un-					
seasoned, 1 cup	345	11	4	65	600	0
Broccoli stalks, 1 cup	40	4	0	8	30	0
Brussel Sprouts, cooked,					
drained, 1 cup	55	7	1	10	16	0
Butter, unsalted, 1 Tbsp.	100	0	11	0	0	36
Butter, unsalted,					
whipped, 1 Tbsp.	75	0	9	0	0	29
Cabbage, Chinese, 1 lb.	62	5.3	.4	15	101	0
Cabbage, regular, 1 lb.	98	5.3	.8	22	82	0
Cabbage, fresh,					
shredded, 1 cup	22	1.2	Trace	4.9	20	0
Carrots, fresh, 1 med.	30	.8	.1	7	30	0
Cauliflower, fresh or					
frozen, ½ cup	14	1.4	.2	2.5	6	0
Celery, 1 stalk	7	Trace	Trace	2	50	0
Cheese, Cheddar, 1 oz.	113	7.1	7.1	.6	176	30
Cheese, Cottage, 1% fat,					
½ cup	90	14	1	4	10	5
Cheese, Whey, less than					
1% fat, ½ cup	80	13	1	4	10	5
Cherries, fresh, 10 med.	47	.9	.2	12	0	0
Chicken, White,					
boneless, cooked,					
3 oz.	150	28	3	0	75	65
Chicken Breast, raw,					
½ lb.	300	48	6	0	160	140
Chicken Stock, salt &					
fat-free, 1 cup	12	1	1	0	Trace	0
Clams, raw, meat only,					
4 oz. (18 med.)	90	13	2	2	266	47
Clams, in shell, 12 med.	104	16	2.1	1.4	370	194

Coconut, fresh, ½ cup	225	3	23	6	1.2	0
Codfish, fresh, fillet, 4 oz.	90	20	.5	0	80	57
Corn on the cob, 5″ 1 ear	70	2.5	.8	16	Trace	0
Cornmeal, (degerminated) 3 Tbsp.	100	2	1	22	10	0
Cornstarch, 1 Tbsp.	30	0	0	7	Trace	0
Cucumbers, 1 med. (8″ long)	20	8	0	4.5	0	0
Egg, whole, 1	75	7	5	0	53	220
Egg, white, 1	17	3.6	0	0	48	0
Eggplant, 1 lb.	92	4.4	.7	20.6	0	0
Flounder, flesh only, 4 oz.	90	19	.9	0	88	57
Flour, whole wheat, 1 Tbsp.	29	1	.1	6.5	0	0
Flour, whole wheat, 1 cup	420	13.6	1.5	84	2	0
Gelatin, unflavored, 1 Tbsp. (1 packet)	25	6	0	0	0	0
Grapefruit, ½ med.	40	.5	0	10	1	0
Grapes, Thompson, 10	35	Trace	Trace	9.1	0	0
Green Beans, fresh, 1 cup	30	2	Trace	7	7	0
Haddock, flesh only, uncooked, 4 oz.	90	22	Trace	0	65	75
Halibut, flesh only, uncooked, 4 oz.	113	23.7	1.5	0	61	70
Honey, 1 Tbsp.	64	1	0	17	0	0
Honeydew, ½ lb.	47	1.2	.4	11	17	0
Horseradish, 1 oz.	11	0	0	3	33	0
Jelly, all flavors, 1 Tbsp.	49	0	0	13	0	0

Food						
Lamb, rib, 26% fat, choice-grade, ¼ lb.	27	15	23	0	70	81
Lasagna, 1 oz. dry	210	7	1	41	3	0
Lemon, 1 med.	20	.8	Trace	5	0	0
Lemon Juice, ¼ cup	15	0	0	4	0	0
Lentils, cooked, 1 cup	210	16	Trace	39	0	0
Lettuce, 1 lb. head	47	4	.7	6.7	30	0
Lime, 1 med.	20	0	0	5	0	0
Liver, Beef, uncooked, 4 oz.	155	22	4	6	155	340
Liver, Chicken, uncooked, 4 oz.	145	22	4	3	80	300
Liver, Calf, 4 oz.	155	22	5	5	85	325
Lobster, raw, 1 lb.	107	19.9	2.2	.6	Not available	235
Lobster, raw, flesh only, 4 oz.	104	19.9	2.2	.5	Not available	225
Macaroni, cooked, 1 cup	192	6.5	.7	37	1	0
Margarine, stick, salt-free, 1 Tbsp.	102	0	11	0	0	0
Margarine, whipped, 1 Tbsp.	69	0	7.5	0	0	0
Mayonnaise, 1 Tbsp.	101	.2	11	.3	84	10
Melon, Cantaloupe, ½ med. (1 lb.)	68	1.6	.2	17	27	0
Milk, Buttermilk, skim, low fat, 1 cup	90	9	Trace	12	320	0
Milk, Evaporated, skim, canned, ½ cup	96	9	Trace	12	165	0
Milk, Skim, 1 Tbsp.	5	.5	Trace	2	8	1
Milk, Skim, 1 cup	90	9	Trace	12	125	5
Milk, 2% fat, 1 cup	140	8.5	5	12	150	22
Milk, Whole, 1 cup	159	8.5	8.5	12	122	34
Mozzarella Cheese, whole milk, 1 oz.	90	6	7	1	27	N.A.
Mushrooms, ½ cup	10	.9	0	2	0	0
Mussels, in the shell, 1 lb.	125	18	2.9	4.3	380	40
Mustard, Dijon, 1 tsp.	4	Trace	Trace	1	70	0
Mustard, Regular, 1 tsp.	3	Trace	Trace	1	58	0

Nectarine, fresh, 1 med.	55	Trace	0	12	5	0
Noodles, egg noodles, cooked, 1 cup	200	7	2	37	4	55
Oatmeal, rolled oats, uncooked, ⅓ cup	110	5	2	18	10	0
Oil: corn, peanut, soy-bean, sesame; 1 Tbsp.	120	0	14	0	0	0
Okra, frozen, ½ cup	35	2.4	Trace	7.6	2	0
Olives, 1 large green	9	Trace	1	Trace	195	0
Onion, sliced, 1 small (½ cup)	22	1	Trace	2.5	10	0
Onion, Green (4)	36	1.5	0	8.2	5	0
Orange, fresh, 1 med.	65	1	Trace	16	0	0
Orange Juice, concen-trate, 6 oz. can	360	5	Trace	87	0	0
Orange, Mandarin (see Tangerine)						
Orange Juice, fresh or frozen, 1 cup	110	2	Trace	26	0	0
Oysters in shell, 1 lb.	30	3.8	.8	1.5	33	90
Oysters, meat only, 4 oz.	75	9.5	2	4	82.7	225
Parmesan Cheese, 1 Tbsp.	25	2	1.5	Trace	88	0
Peaches, fresh, 1 med. (about 4 per lb.)	40	1	Trace	10	1	0
Peaches, halved, water-pack, ½ cup	75	1	Trace	10	1	0
Peanut Butter, without salt, 1 Tbsp.	95	4	8	3	0	0
Peanuts, roasted, in shell,10 med.	105	4.7	8.8	3.7	0	0
Pears, fresh, Bartlett, 1 med.	100	1	1	25	2	0
Pears, canned, halved, water-pack, ½ pear	39	Trace	Trace	10	0	0
Peas, canned, drained, 1 cup	150	8	1	29	690	0
Pepper, fresh (4 to a lb.), green, 1 med.	22	1.2	Trace	4.8	13	0

Pepper, fresh, red, 1 med.	31	1.4	Trace	7.1	0	0

Pineapple, chunks or
  crushed, canned in
  its own juice, 1 cup
	140	1	1	35	0	0

Pineapple, canned,
  sliced, own juice,
  1 slice
	35	Trace	Trace	8.7	0	0

Pineapple, fresh, 3½" slice	44	Trace	Trace	11	0	0
Plums, Italian, 1	20	Trace	Trace	5	0	0
Potato, fresh, 1 lb.	280	7.7	Trace	62.8	11	0
Prunes, dried, uncooked, unsweetened, 5 large	110	1	Trace	29	3	0
Raisins, 1 Tbsp.	25	0	0	6	3	0
Raspberries, red, fresh, ½ cup	35	.8	Trace	9	0	0
Raspberries, red, frozen, ½ cup	123	.9	.2	31	0	0
Rhubarb, fresh, diced, 1 cup	18	.6	Trace	4	2	0
Rice, brown, uncooked, 1 cup	800	17	4	175	20	0
Rice, brown, cooked, 1 cup	230	5	1.2	50	Trace	0
Rolls, whole wheat, 1 med.	105	4	1.1	19	250	0
Rum, 1½ oz.	100					
Salmon, red, canned, 1 lb.	953	88.9	63	0	1560	0
Salmon, fresh, 4 oz.	240	24.5	13.7	0	50	55
Salt, 1 tsp.	0	0	0	0	2325	0
Scallops, meat only, uncooked, 4 oz.	90	17	0	5	255	60
Sesame Seeds, 1 Tbsp., (½ oz.)	80	2.5	7	3	8.5	0
Shrimp, uncooked, shelled, 4 oz.	105	20	1	1	158	161

Sole, Flounder, raw fillet 1 lb.	358	75.8	3	0	354	236
Swordfish, uncooked, fresh, 4 oz.	134	21.7	4.5	0	N.A.	88
Spaghetti, cooked, 1 cup	155	5	1	32	10	0
Spinach, frozen, 1 cup	45	6	1	8	130	0
Spinach, fresh, 1 cup	15	2	Trace	2	24	0
Squash, Summer, 1 med. (½ lb.)	38	2.2	Trace	8.4	2	0
Squash, Winter, ½ (about ½ lb.)	100	2.8		25	Trace	0
Starch, Arrowroot, 1 Tbsp.	30	0	0	7	0	0
Starch, Corn, 1 Tbsp.	30	0	0	7	0	0
Strawberries, fresh, 1 cup	55	1	.7	13	0	0
Sugar, White, granulated, 1 Tbsp.	48	0	0	12	0	0
Sugar, White, granulated, 1 cup	770	0	0	190	0	0
Sugar, Brown, 1 cup	820	0	0	205	0	0
Sunflower seeds, shelled, 1 oz.	80	3.3	6.6	2.8	4.2	0
Sweet Potatoes, fresh, 1 med. (4 to a lb.)	120	2	Trace	28	10	0
Syrup, Maple, 1 Tbsp.	50	0	0	13	0	0
Tangerine, 1 med.	39	.7	Trace	10	0	0
Tomatoes, canned, 1 lb.	95	4	1	20	580	0
Tomato Catsup 1 Tbsp.	18	Trace	Trace	4	175	0
Tomatoes, fresh, 1 med.	27	1.4	0	5.2	4	0
Tomato Juice, canned, 1 cup	46	2.2	Trace	10	245	0
Tomato paste, 1 can, 6 oz.	139	5.8	.7	32	80	0
Tomato Puree, 1 cup	110	5	Trace	23	998	0
Tomato Sauce, 8 oz.	80	3	16	1	1296	0
Tuna, 7 oz. can, water-pack	252	56	16	0	800	56
Turkey, 3 oz., light meat, no skin	150	28	3	0	70	68

Turkey, Roasted, dark meat only, no skin	175	26	7	0	86	87
Veal, Loin fillet, 15% fat, 4 oz.	205	22.3	12.5	0	Trace	90
Vermouth, 3½ oz.	105					
Vinegar, 1 cup	30	0	0	7	0	0
Water Chestnuts, canned, 4 oz.	85	1.7	0	22	0	0
Walnuts, shelled, ½ cup	392	13	36	8	0	0
Watermelon, fresh, 1 lb.	53	1	Trace	13.4	2	0
Wheat Germ, ¼ cup or 1 oz.	110	9	3	13	100	0
Whey Cheese, 1% fat, 1 cup	160	24	3	8	128	0
Wine, white or red, dry, 3½ oz.	90	0	0		6	0
Yogurt, homemade, skim, 1 cup	90	9	0	12	125	6
Yogurt, partially skimmed milk, 1 cup	123	8.3	4.2	13	125	16
Yogurt, whole milk, 1 cup	152	7.4	8.3	12	125	N.A.
Zucchini, raw, sliced, 1 cup	20	2	0	3.5	2	0

baddie list

Food	Calories	Protein	Fat	Carbohydrate	Sodium	Cholesterol
Bacon, 2 slices, crisp, fried	90	5	8	1	165	70
Chocolate Layer Cake, frudge frosting, 2″ wedge	360	3.8	16.4	55	235	42
Chocolate Cookies, chip, 5 med.	235	5.4	21	70	400	4
Ice cream, 3½ oz. scoop	210	4	12.5	20.5	40	45
Ice milk, 3½ oz. scoop	156	4.8	5.1	22	68	22
Italian dressing, 2 Tbsp.	160	0	18	0	630	0
Liverwurst, 2 oz.	175	9	15	1	499	0
Peanuts, salted, roasted (8-10)	53	2.3	4.5	1.7	40	0
Pie: apple, peach, pineapple, cherry, 3½″ slice	305	2.6	13	45	300	0
Pie, Pecan, 3½″ slice	431	5.3	24	53	300	0
Pie, Pumpkin, 3½″ slice	241	4.6	13	28	320	0

The food values in these charts have been abstracted from *Composition of Foods — Raw, Processed, Prepared.* Agricultural Handbook No. 8, and *Nutritive Value of Foods,* Home and Garden Bulletin No. 72. Both booklets are published by the United States Department of Agriculture, Washington, D.C.

bibliography

Books:

Brewster, Letitia and Jacobson, Michael F.: *The Changing American Diet.* Center for Science in the Public Interest, Washington, D.C. 20009, 1978.

Burton, Benjamin T.: *Human Nutrition,* 3rd edition. McGraw-Hill, New York, 1976.

Fredyberg, Nicholas and Gortner, Willis: *The Food Additives Book,* Bantam Books, New York, 1982.

Stunkard, Albert J., M.D., editor: *Obesity.* W.B. Saunders Co., Philadelphia, 1980.

Tobias, Alice L. And Thompson, Patricia J.: *Issues in Nutrition for the 1980's.* Wadsworth Health Science Division, Monterey, CA, 1980.

White, Philip L., Fletcher, Dean C., Ellis, Mary: *Nutrients in Processed Foods.* Publishing Sciences Group Inc., Acton, MA, 1975.

Winich, Myron: *Nutrition and the Killer Diseases.* John Wiley and Sons, New York, 1981.

Yudkin, John: *Sweet and Dangerous.* Peter H. Wydin, Inc., New York, 1972.

Magazines & Reports:

Cholesterol: You Can't Win: Science News 119:55, January 24, 1981

Caffeine: How to Consume Less: Consumer Reports, October 1981, 597-99.

Dietary Goals for the United States: 2nd. ed., Report of the Select Committee on Nutrition and Human Needs, U.S. Senate. U.S. Government Printing Office, Washington, DC 1977.

Prudent Diet for Children?: G.B. Kolath, *Science* 211:912, February 27, 1981.

New Strength in the Diet-Disease Link?: W.J. Broad, *Science* 206:666-8, November 9, 1979.

Recommended Dietary Allowances: 8th ed., Food and Nutrition Board, National Research Council, National Academy of Sciences, Washington, D 1974.

Salt and High Blood Pressure: Consumer Reports, 44, March 1979, 144.

general index

main dishes

stocks

vegetables

notes

notes

notes

PHOTO: FERN MATTHEWS

The authors
FLORENCE MATTHEWS
and
FLORENCE KULICK
(left to right)

FLORENCE MATTHEWS has a Masters Degree in Home Economics with a major in Nutrition from Teachers College, Columbia University. She taught home economics and nutrition for twenty years and is a member of the Society for Nutritional Education. For the past fifteen years she has been investigating the latest nutritional and medical research and applying these principles in developing diets for weight loss and healthful living.

FLORENCE KULICK has a B.S. in Community Service from Stony Brook, S.U.N.Y. She also attended classes at Columbia University and Queens College in New York. She started cooking as a child of eight and published her first recipes a few years later in her school newspaper. She writes restaurant reviews for a Long Island publication. She is the mother of three, grandmother of four, and lives with her husband, Bernard, in their East Hampton house.

Together the authors taught their nutritional cuisine to adults at Southampton College, to community groups and on local cable TV. They also do lecture-demonstrations at hospitals and before health educators.